"Thinking about pursuing National Board Certification in World Languages, but not sure where to start? Look no further than this clearly laid out, often hilarious primer! The authors' expertise shines through the pages—there are many reflective questions sprinkled throughout every chapter, as well as personal anecdotes from their own classrooms. As someone who loves checklists, I was delighted to see the comprehensive approach to completing every component. If you are searching for a friend to hold your hand as you complete the process, buy this book!"

Heather Tedder, *National Board Certified Teacher since 2010, PhD candidate in French and Francophone Studies at Louisiana State University, 2020 NC World Language Teacher of the Year*

"A straightforward and practical guide that gives you clear instructions for the hard but career-changing work of becoming an NBCT."

Liz Matchett, *Executive Director, California Language Teachers' Association, Stanford Teacher Education Program Lecturer, National Board Certified Teacher since 2005*

"This book is a no-nonsense approach to National Boards in World Languages that embodies 'clear is kind'—no sugar-coating, just honest guidance about a transformative journey. The authors don't suggest that it will be easy but they promise it will be worth it. This is both a guidebook and a workbook that informs what it really takes to achieve National Board Certification."

Thomas Soth, *Past President of The Foreign Language Association of NC and the Southern Conference on Language Teaching, AP Spanish Language and Culture and AP Spanish Literature and Culture Consultant, National Board Certified Teacher since 2006*

"This book is an essential resource for any world language educator pursuing National Board Certification. The authors break down all four components in a way that is both clear and approachable, taking what can feel like an overwhelming process and making it manageable. It is a great guide for anyone on this journey and will serve as a trusted guide from start to finish."

Mirta Valdés-Bradner, *National Board Certified Teacher, North Caroline High School, Maryland, Maryland Foreign Language Association 2024 Language Educator of the Year, Fund For Teachers Fellow 2025*

"The authors have masterfully captured the spirit of National Board Certification for World Languages in this invaluable guide. From start to finish, the book delivers a clear, practical breakdown of the entire reflective process. The detailed explanations of each component, paired with the interactive "Your Turn!" segments, make you feel like you're part of the book and set you up for a reflection journey throughout each chapter. This resource is sure to be a trusted companion for any World Language teacher pursuing certification. I only wish a book this thorough and supportive had existed when I completed my own initial certification!"

Carmen Scoggins, *National Board Certified Teacher in Spanish since 2010 and renewed in 2019, Past President of The Foreign Language Association of NC and the Southern Conference on Language Teaching, ACTFL Award for Excellence in World Language Instruction Using Technology (K-12) 2015, ACTFL Florence Steiner Award for Leadership in World Language Education (K-12) 2020*

Achieving National Board Certification in World Languages

Achieving National Board Certification in World Languages is the essential companion for World Language teachers who are currently working on, or considering working on, the National Board Certified Teacher (NBCT) process with the National Board for Professional Teaching Standards (NBPTS).

Written by two secondary teachers who are both NBCTs, the book provides candidates with support and guidance through the process of obtaining National Board Certification, as many candidates in world language certify alone without a mentor teacher. The process to become an NBCT is rigorous, and there is minimal support available to help teachers through this process. This book offers a solution to this as an in-hand and in-print mentor for candidates. Case studies and Your Turn segments provide space to brainstorm, plan, and measure the candidate's work against the National Board rubrics. This book will ensure candidates can have greater peace of mind that they submitted the best possible portfolio and that they responded to the prompts in the way that most accurately reflects accomplished teaching.

This is an essential resource for secondary World Language teachers who are working on or considering National Board Certification.

Erin E. H. Austin is a National Board Certified French teacher, a 2018 NEA Foundation Global Fellow, and the Colorado Congress of Foreign Language Teachers' 2023 Teacher of the Year.

Lisa Bartels is a National Board Certified Teacher and the 2023 Teacher of the Year for the Foreign Language Association of North Carolina. She is a veteran teacher with over 20 years of classroom experience on three continents.

Also Available from Routledge Eye On Education
(www.routledge.com/eyeoneducation)

Going Global in the World Language Classroom: Ideas, Strategies, and Resources for Teaching and Learning With the World
Erin E. H. Austin

The Ultimate Guide to Selling Your Original World Language Resources: How to Open, Fill, and Grow a Successful Online Curriculum Store
Erin E. H. Austin

Teaching Multilingual Students Through Culture and Language: An Elementary Teacher's Guide to Self-Discovery Using Semiotics
Tala Michelle Karkar-Esperat

Building Proficiency for World Language Learners: 100+ High-Interest Activities
Janina Klimas

Teaching World Languages with the Five Senses: Practical Strategies and Ideas for Hands-On Learning
Elizabeth Porter

Differentiated Instruction: A Guide for World Language Teachers, 3rd edition
Deborah Blaz

Sparking Creativity in the World Language Classroom: Strategies and Ideas to Build Your Students' Language Skills
Deborah Blaz and Tom Alsop

Achieving National Board Certification in World Languages

Proven Strategies and Tips for Accomplished Teaching

Erin E. H. Austin and Lisa Bartels

NEW YORK AND LONDON

Designed cover image: © Getty Images

First published 2026
by Routledge
605 Third Avenue, New York, NY 10158

and by Routledge
4 Park Square, Milton Park, Abingdon, Oxon, OX14 4RN

Routledge is an imprint of the Taylor & Francis Group, an informa business

© 2026 Erin E. H. Austin and Lisa Bartels

The right of Erin E. H. Austin and Lisa Bartels to be identified as authors of this work has been asserted in accordance with sections 77 and 78 of the Copyright, Designs and Patents Act 1988.

All rights reserved. The purchase of this copyright material confers the right on the purchasing institution to photocopy or download pages which bear a copyright line at the bottom of the page. No other parts of this book may be reprinted or reproduced or utilised in any form or by any electronic, mechanical, or other means, now known or hereafter invented, including photocopying and recording, or in any information storage or retrieval system, without permission in writing from the publishers.

For Product Safety Concerns and Information please contact our EU representative GPSR@taylorandfrancis.com. Taylor & Francis Verlag GmbH, Kaufingerstraße 24, 80331 München, Germany.

Trademark notice: Product or corporate names may be trademarks or registered trademarks, and are used only for identification and explanation without intent to infringe.

ISBN: 978-1-041-20537-1 (hbk)
ISBN: 978-1-041-20535-7 (pbk)
ISBN: 978-1-003-71686-0 (ebk)

DOI: 10.4324/9781003716860

Typeset in Palatino
by KnowledgeWorks Global Ltd.

Access the Support Material: https://resourcecentre.routledge.com/books/9781041205357

*For all NBC candidates.
Everything you do for students matters.*

Table of Contents

Acknowledgments xi
Meet the Authors xiii
Introduction xv

SECTION 1
BEFORE YOU BEGIN 1

1 Starting Your Journey 3

2 Planning Your Portfolio. 11

3 A Specific Kind of Writing 21

4 Bookends: Knowledge of Students and
   Reflection 29

5 Common Overall Pitfalls 41

SECTION 2
THE FOUR COMPONENTS 51

6 Component 1: Content Knowledge. 53

7 Component 2: Differentiation in Instruction 93

8 Component 3: Teaching Practice and Learning
   Environment 123

9 Component 4: Effective and Reflective
   Practitioner. 147

SECTION 3
WHAT'S NEXT? 191

10 After Submitting Your Portfolio 193

11 Maintenance of Certification 201

Glossary 215
Resources. 219

Acknowledgments

From Both of Us: We could not have written this book without professional input from the many teachers across the country who responded to our surveys. Our work was deeply enriched by the input of Victoria Funk, Derick Flores, and Cecilia Camarero, who generously shared their knowledge of Spanish and of their home cultures of Colombia, Honduras, and Argentina. Lastly, no one would be holding this book if it wasn't for our editor, Megha Patel, believing in it and patiently answering all of our (hundreds of) questions.

From Erin: I could never write anything if it wasn't for Daryl, Emmett, and Everly supporting my visions and being able to fend for themselves while I write! I'm also so grateful to Lisa Showers, Kristy Bibbey, Elissa Pitts, and Marcy Lewis for being such wonderful support to me while I navigated my initial National Board Certification.

From Lisa: My love and thanks to Maggie, Ryan, Grace, and Katherine for serving as guinea pigs, pop culture advisors, and providers of ruthlessly honest feedback on all my crazy ideas. I am indebted to many colleagues who encouraged me on my NBC journey, especially Blake Norby, David Lovin, and Shelby Cole. And my deepest gratitude to Mike for cheerfully encouraging my obsession with instructional practice for almost three decades!

Meet the Authors

Erin E. H. Austin is a National Board Certified French teacher in Colorado and the 2023 Teacher of the Year for the Colorado Congress of Foreign Language Teachers. She holds a B.A. in both French and Art Education, a M.A. in Curriculum & Instruction, and graduate certificates in French Studies and Gifted, Creative, & Talented Education. A 2018 NEA Foundation Global Learning Fellow, she now presents nationally on global education topics and supports the NEA Foundation as a grant reviewer. In addition to doing contract writing work, Ms. Austin is the author of *The Ultimate Guide to Selling Your Original World Language Resources: How to Open, Fill, and Grow a Successful Online Curriculum Store* (Routledge, 2021), and *Going Global in the World Language Classroom: Ideas, Strategies, and Resources for Teaching and Learning With the World* (Routledge, 2023). She has been a featured guest on many education podcasts, regularly mentors National Board Certification candidates, and currently serves on the board of the Abundant Yoga Community, a non-profit in western Wisconsin whose mission is to bring yoga to those with financial or geographic barriers. Outside of work, she is most often globe-trotting with family and friends, planning her next trip, or recovering from the last trip … with a healthy amount of reading and rescue pup snuggling mixed in.

Erin Austin

Lisa Bartels is a National Board Certified Teacher and the 2023 Teacher of the Year for the Foreign Language Association of North Carolina. A veteran teacher with over 20 years of classroom experience on three continents, Ms. Bartels holds a B.A. in French and a M.Ed. in Curriculum and Instruction. She serves on the board of the Foreign Language Association of North Carolina, is past president of the North Carolina chapter of the American Association of Teachers of French, and was honored as the 2023 AATF Outstanding Chapter Officer. Ms. Bartels is a frequent presenter at professional conferences and is active in educational consulting, mentoring, curriculum writing, and promoting world language instruction. She shares tips and resources for classroom teachers on her blog, www.explorecurriculum.com. When she is not teaching or writing curriculum, Ms. Bartels loves hiking, camping, and kayaking with her husband and four children.

Lisa Bartels

Introduction

Welcome to the process of becoming a National Board Certified Teacher (NBCT) with the National Board for Professional Teaching Standards (NBPTS)! And, incidentally, welcome to a new batch of education-related acronyms!

The most effective way to introduce you to this book and journey is with what we feel is arguably the most important quote about Board Certification that we've encountered:

> No one begins this process as a National Board Certified Teacher; it's the process that makes you become one.

It is truly the *process* that is the most valuable and, unfortunately, that is easy to lose sight of when you're in the thick of it. When we start teaching, no one nails it in Year 1. For most people, it takes a solid five years—and often more!—to finally feel like we're in any sort of groove and even *somewhat* feel like we know what we're doing. We're simply not born into 100% pedagogical competency. Likewise, we're not born NBCTs. It takes candidates different amounts of time to get into the groove of what's required to become proficient in the Architecture of Accomplished Teaching set forth by the NBPTS. Whatever your pace is, know that you're not alone and that you're moving forward.

Our Goal

Our primary goal is to support candidates in becoming NBCTs. We hope this book functions as a portable mentor, a guide you can return to again and again as you navigate the process of becoming an NBCT. With any luck, it'll end up battered and beaten, dog-eared and drink-stained, littered with Post-It flags… and helpful.

Who Are the Authors

If our goal is for this book to be a mentor to you, it's important that we establish a relationship. Who we are, what we bring to the table, and why we're here matters in that foundation.

> **Erin:** I am a National Board Certified Teacher in French, but I am also dual-certified in art. As of this publication date, I'm in my 24th year of teaching … and still loving it! Those 24 years include teaching elementary art, junior high French and art, high school French (including concurrent enrollment and International Baccalaureate), and AP Art History. I initially certified as a NBCT in 2019, and I have since maintained certification. As a full-time teacher and author of two other books for world language teachers, I present at world language conferences across the U.S., including sessions on the NBPTS certification process. I share information and tips for world language teachers working on certification on my YouTube channel and website (www.onygomadame.com), and I do private mentoring for NBCT candidates.

> **Lisa:** I earned my National Board Certification in French in 2017, have since maintained certification, and I have served as a NBPTS scorer. I also hold a certification in Spanish and (formerly) in 6-12 English Language Arts. My 22 years of teaching includes two years in an international school in Cameroon, Africa, and eight years in the Philippines, teaching almost every imaginable combination of middle and high school languages. Like many of you, I've experienced the challenges of juggling multiple preps and operating without adequate curriculum, resources, or support. All of this motivates me to invest in my colleagues through professional development presentations, my blog (www.explorecurriculum.com), and as a mentor for new teachers and NBCT candidates.

If it seems like we may be super nerds who have no lives, you're half right! Super language nerds? Check! Professional development junkies? Check, yet again! More importantly, however, is the fact that we both truly believe in the power of the *process* of becoming an NBCT. Without a doubt, we know that we are personally better teachers because of it, and we know our students have benefited.

The impact isn't solely limited to us and to our students, however. In fact, the NBPTS reports that years of research show "students of Board-certified teachers learn more than their peers without Board-certified teachers" and "91% of teachers engaging with the National Board standards reported that it had a direct impact on their instructional practices." Additionally, it's compelling to note that the National Board process was created *by teachers*. We all know what it's like to pinch ourselves to stay awake during professional development sessions delivered by presenters who simply don't get it because they aren't one of us. National Board certification (NBC), by contrast, is for us, by us.

> The NBCT process was an affirmation of what I was doing well, and what I wasn't doing well. For all of the entries (and renewal) you must reflect on what you do, why you do it, and why it impacts student achievement. This reflective process I have tried to implement in everything I do in the classroom, from new activities to my unit planning. —Shelby Cole, NBCT since 2011

What Is in This Book

We made this book into a combination of everything we wished we had when we were certifying and everything we have repeatedly seen while mentoring or reviewing for the NBPTS. Over the course of several years, we amassed quite a list of common threads—issues that, with a mentor, are much more easily solvable. Based directly on these trends, we have included several helpful elements in this book:

- ♦ **Your Turn! Workbook sections.** We cannot underscore the importance of proper planning enough! Both of us have worked with candidates who failed to adequately plan and reflect at various stages of this process. We don't want that to happen to you, so we built in space for you to plan right within the pages of this text. We recommend that you use the space provided to jot down ideas, to map out your plan, and to check the work you've done. Alternatively, if you can't bring yourself to write in a book (fair enough!), use your own notebook or electronic document companion to this book to complete the Your Turn! Sections.

- **Case Study Practice and Case Study Analysis sections.** In addition to the Your Turn! workbook sections, you'll also encounter Case Study segments designed to illustrate our points. They are not representative of any real teacher, but rather, they are mash-ups of situations we've encountered. Use these case study examples to practice your understanding of the concepts and strategies presented within the chapter they appear.
- **Writing tips.** Chapter 3 uniquely addresses the kind of writing you'll do, as a whole, in this process. The writing required for successful completion of the NBPTS portfolio isn't necessarily a style that most teachers are familiar with or comfortable with, so don't skip that chapter! Additionally, throughout Section 2, each chapter includes writing tips embedded into the content and specific to the component you are working on.
- **Reminders.** Much of what you will find in this book links to other chapters and to information put forth by the NBPTS. We give reminders to refer to specific chapters, sections, or documents that support what you are reading at any given point.
- **Study tips.** Chapter 6, which focuses on Component 1, is especially full of study tips. Here, we expanded on the (very limited) guidance provided by the NBPTS to create a list of concepts accomplished world language teachers should be familiar with. We also share helpful advice in preparing for the Constructed Response section.

- **Common pitfalls.** Based on our experiences in mentoring and reviewing, these are mistakes we have seen candidates often make, along with tips for avoiding them. Chapters 6–9 include common pitfalls specific to those Components, while Chapter 5 focuses on *overall* pitfalls in the process.
- **Three sections.** Section 1 includes chapters that are necessary for success in the process as a whole. Section 2 includes chapters specific to each of the four NBPTS Components. This section's chapters can feel a bit more intense … but the Components *are* intense. Section 3 addresses what comes after submitting your final Component's work.

What Is Not in This Book

While we strive to make this guide as useful as possible, there are some limits.

- **We don't give formatting tips.** Formatting specifics (e.g., required fonts, margins, page counts, submission requirements) are easily subject to change, and they also don't directly relate to what excites us: *developing as educators*. We prefer to keep this text focused on world language pedagogy and growth, and leave the details to the individual candidates. If you have formatting questions, refer to the NBPTS guides and/or contact the NBPTS directly at 1-800-22TEACH (83224).
- **We don't teach pedagogical content.** Foundational professional elements such as teaching strategies, classroom activities, lesson design, classroom management, and knowledge of your target language and culture are outside the scope of this book. Candidates should be proficient in these areas *before* attempting certification; the process is intended to grow already skilled teachers into accomplished educators, as defined by the NBPTS.

- **We don't give writing examples.** NBPTS intentionally does not provide examples or sample entries, and candidates sign an agreement not to provide their own portfolio entries as models for others. The rationale is that there are *many* ways to demonstrate accomplished teaching, and each candidate should show their professionalism in their own unique way. In this spirit, we have declined to provide any suggested content or sample answers in this book, even though candidates sometimes ask for them. At the end of the day, your portfolio is yours and yours alone!
- **We don't give answers.** For Components 2–4, there are no "right answers"; rather, these components require thoughtful explanation and reflection specific to your teaching and learning context. Component 1, however, does include some "right answers," most specifically within the Selected Response (multiple choice) section. While it's flattering to think that some readers may assume we know the answers, we certainly don't. Even if we did, it would be unethical for us to share them. Each candidate, including the two of us during our respective processes, has to put in the hard work. What we *can* do and *do* do, however, is expand on what the NBPTS states in their guide as topics in which they want successful candidates to be well-versed.
- **We don't replace the NBPTS content.** This book is *supplemental*. It is not meant, in any way, to replace guides and instructions put out by the NBPTS; those should be referred to first and foremost.
- **We don't represent the NBPTS.** All opinions and recommendations in this book are strictly our own. Neither of us are employees of the NBPTS, nor are we acting on its behalf. This book is not approved or endorsed by the NBPTS.

Going forward, we understand the temptation to skip right to Section 2 and to dig into the details of Components 1–4. On the surface, that makes perfect sense! However, we strongly recommend working your way through the chapters in Section 1 first. These chapters provide a necessary foundation for Components 1–4. Through our work with candidates, we have seen how a lack of foresight and a failure to lay a strong foundation of planning often result in fundamental flaws that arise too late to be fixed.

Now take a deep breath, turn the page, and start the journey. Good luck! You got this.

SECTION 1
Before You Begin

1

Starting Your Journey

Buckle Up!

Since you purchased this book, it's reasonable to assume you have either started the process of becoming a National Board Certified Teacher (NBCT) or are strongly considering it. This journey is *long*. It is rigorous and time-intensive. It will push you in ways you can't imagine, and it will force growth. Your fingers will be tired from typing, and your head will hurt from the sheer volume of reflection. At some point, you will cry, scream, collapse in total exhaustion, and consider quitting. (Anecdotal evidence suggests the likelihood of all four is quite high.)

You will also experience positive changes in your teaching practice that couldn't come from any other process. You will notice yourself, your classroom, your lessons, and your students growing. You will fight through failures, small and large, in much the same way that we teach our students to persevere in the face of difficulty, and when you come out the other end, you will feel a seemingly paradoxical mix of total depletion and boundless energy. *You will become a more accomplished teacher*.

If all that sounds painful, wonderful, and wonderfully painful … welcome to the process of becoming an NBCT. Now buckle up!

DOI: 10.4324/9781003716860-2

Tough Love

Research Professor and Author Brené Brown popularized the phrase "Clear is kind," and it has seeped into the 2000s cultural zeitgeist. Marriage therapists teach spouses that "Clear is kind" when expressing what we want, bosses take on a "Clear is kind" philosophy with employees, and as writers of this book, we want to be absolutely clear with you about the process of National Board Certification (NBC).

So far, we hope to have made these two points clear: First, becoming an NBCT is hard work; second, the hard work is worth it. But there's more to this story of clear, tough love.

Earning the distinction NBCT isn't a formality or a guarantee. There are some programs in education—and, we assume, in most professions—that fall under the category of "hoop jumping." If you jump through the hoops A–C, then you will achieve X. We cannot stress this enough: This is not one of those programs. Rather, it's a process that *will* make you uncomfortable at times. It's not uncommon to, at a minimum, feel frustration; it is also not uncommon to question everything you do, believe, and *are* as a teacher. It is hard work to be introspective and humble and to be prepared to radically shift your practice.

The pass rate statistics make it harder still. Those statistics shift from year to year, but when we certified, the pass rate (on the first time through the process) was approximately 40%. Candidates must take this into consideration. No candidate is *entitled* to passing scores because of who they are, who they know, their degrees, or how long they have taught.

When candidates consider the intensity of the process, there may be some who look for the easy way out, just like some students: "I'll just save myself time and use artificial intelligence (AI) to write my reflections." Again, clear is kind: This process is for teachers looking to grow. If that is not you, this isn't the right professional step. If the NBPTS catches a candidate using AI in a non-approved way, and that candidate's submission is thrown out, that's an expensive lesson to learn!

Additionally, we believe that in this journey—and in life!— *integrity matters*. When Lisa was completing her initial NBC portfolio, she was advised by a colleague to forge evidence. Although it would have been easy to whip up the "perfect parent quote," this is simply *not okay*, and if you get caught, it's costly. Even if you don't get caught, the portfolio isn't really yours, and you will have to live with that knowledge. (Talk about imposter syndrome!) Do the work to the best of your ability, and reach out for support from people or in groups that you trust.

It's not all scary, though! On the contrary, the joy candidates feel when they pass and receive the famous "fireworks message" is significant. It's also essential to note that the *journey* is worthwhile. With or without a finished portfolio submission and with or without the fireworks, this process will strengthen your instructional practice in a way that stretches you into a more accomplished educator. You will be more effective as a result, and that will have a positive impact on students.

Here is what some current NBCTs have to say about the process:

> Since the process is so rigorous, it brings extra pride upon achievement. I can say I rose to the challenge and accomplished something great in my career.
> —Zosha Darnell, NBCT since 2024

> Becoming an NBCT changed me professionally because I learned to self-reflect on whether or not my teaching efforts were increasing student achievement in my classroom and how was I measuring and monitoring that continued student progress of achievement. Becoming an NBCT also changed me personally because the process gave me the confidence and focus to push through and accomplish any task, project, or learning curve that I choose to finish.
> -—Lisa Showers, NBCT since 2003

> I definitely have learned how to adapt my lessons to new ideas or challenges since the first time I got certified. Somehow, my lessons have become more engaging and I'm always seeking for ways to connect students' needs to advantages of learning a foreign language.
> —Gabriela Anaya, NBCT since 2005

In other words, it's common for candidates to agree that the process of becoming a National Board Certified Teacher is a huge challenge … but to also agree that the challenge is worth it!

Calendar Talk

Another vital step in figuring out your path to becoming an NBCT is understanding the scheduling.

Let's start with a common question from prospective candidates: When should I tackle this in my career? First, ask yourself if you meet these NBPTS requirements:

- Do I have a bachelor's degree from an accredited school?
- Do I have a class I could work with that has at least six students, over half of whom are ages 11–18?
- Do I teach a language in which the NBPTS is currently offering certification?
- Do I have a valid teaching license in my state?
- Have I taught for at least three years?
- Do I meet the American Council on the Teaching of Foreign Languages (ACTFL) language proficiency requirements?

If you meet the first five requirements, we recommend taking the ACTFL oral and written proficiency tests (often referred to as the "Hidden Component 5") before starting Components 1–4. The reason is simple: If you are unable to reach the language proficiency requirements, you are ineligible for Components 1–4. From a financial standpoint, these tests are also cheaper than the four NBPTS components, so it's in your best interest to pass the cheapest requirement first.

The proficiency tests consist of two parts: the Oral Proficiency Interview (OPI) and the Writing Proficiency Test (WPT). These tests are scheduled independently of the NBPTS, and candidates must earn an Advanced-Low (or higher) proficiency rating on both tests in order to achieve the NBCT distinction. Because dates, requirements, and duration of score validity can fluctuate, please consult your NBPTS guide to determine how long your scores are valid and when you need to submit them.

After successfully passing the OPI and WPT, it's time to consider Components 1–4 and how they can fit into your life. The components at a glance:

- Component 1 is a test consisting of a multiple choice section and an essay section. It is designed to test your knowledge of the language, of pedagogy, and of the cultures that speak your target language. This component is 40% of your total portfolio score; 20% is the multiple choice, and the remaining 20% is equally divided among three essays.
- Component 2 requires you to focus on two different students in the same class. It is designed to evaluate your skill in designing assessments and in differentiating instruction. This component is 15% of your total portfolio score.
- Component 3 requires two video-recorded lessons showing at least two different lesson formats. It is designed to showcase pedagogy in practice. This component is 30% of your total portfolio score.
- Component 4 requires you to identify two different needs: a professional need for yourself and a need your students have. These two needs can be related or unrelated. You will show how you pursued professional development, sought out resources, and collaborated with a variety of stakeholders to meet both needs, leading to student growth. This component is 15% of your total portfolio score.

Each component is similar to a graduate course in terms of time and energy. How many graduate courses could you complete in a school year, given your current professional and personal demands? The answer to that question is a sensible guideline for how many components you could reasonably submit per year.

It's not uncommon for candidates to ask, "Can I do all four components in one year?" Well, do you value your sanity? (Now, it's possible you are a middle school teacher, and sanity has waved "bye bye" to you long ago, so our question clearly is relative!) The level of scrutiny you're applying to your teaching practice during your NBCT candidacy is so intense that it's difficult to maintain while teaching. Therefore, for the majority of candidates, we advise against doing all four components in one year. Many candidates find 1–2 components per year is the sweet spot for balancing both momentum and sanity.

NBCT candidates absolutely take different routes to the same destination, so after completing the ACTFL proficiency tests, we recommend continuing with Component 1. The rationale is that this component is completed in a single day, and it's weighted more heavily (40% at the time of publication) in the scoring. It's a one-and-done type of component, and that can give a good momentum boost for going forward.

If you're hoping to complete two components in a single year, we recommend starting with Components 1 and 2 (after passing the ACTFL tests) in year one, continuing to Components 3 and 4 in year two, and then redoing any components that you may need to after that. This pace (often, not always) is slow enough to keep candidates from being completely overwhelmed but aggressive enough that candidates can see the light at the end of the tunnel and maintain momentum.

Finally, consider when in your career this process best fits … and there is no right answer here! It can be beneficial to have been teaching long enough to feel like you're in a flow, and you (mostly) know what you're doing. In other words, start when your basic teaching and curriculum are nailed down. The NBCT process is going to take a lot of time, so it's good if some areas of your job are on autopilot when you start.

It can also be advantageous to start at a time when you feel ready to shake things up a bit and challenge your professional practice *because* you have a good professional flow going. It would interrupt a professional flow, however, if you are teaching an Advanced Placement (AP) or International Baccalaureate (IB) class for the first time or have another large professional change taking place. If that's the case, we recommend waiting until you have a more established rhythm.

Erin started her 2-year NBC process after teaching for 15 years. In year one of her NBC journey, she had a toddler; in year two, she was pregnant; and a week or two after submitting her final components, she gave birth. (Crazy? Perhaps, but her rationale was that it was not going to get *easier* when there were more kids to chase!) Lisa began working on her NBC upon returning to the U.S. after teaching abroad for 12 years. She had four elementary and middle school children, and NBC became a family affair; her husband handled the meal prep, and her kids took on extra household responsibilities to free up time for Mom to research and write. When those iconic fireworks appeared on the screen, the whole family celebrated!

The Buddy System

Many candidates find success with a buddy system approach (i.e., navigating the process with a colleague or friend). There are a few variations of this, all of which can be successful:

- Join a group. There are a variety of NBCT candidate support groups on social media platforms, and one active group is "National Board Certification for World Language Teachers" on Facebook. In a group, candidates can pose questions to get ideas, clarification, and encouragement from others going through the process, as well as from current NBCTs.
- Tackle certification with another teacher. If you have a world language colleague who is also interested in becoming an NBCT, how lucky! Dig in, and chart a "plan of attack" calendar together. But not everyone works with another language teacher in their building, and even for those who do, not every language teacher is interested. In that case, consider reaching out to your state world language teacher organization and asking if there's anyone interested in working through certification together. It is also worth noting that *any* strong and accomplished teacher, even one outside your discipline, can be a valuable partner.

- Find a mentor. Free social media-based groups are fantastic, but you can also use those groups to find NBCTs who would be happy to provide 1:1 direct support to a candidate. It is possible to find someone willing to mentor you for free, but if you have more than an hour's worth of work planned for a mentor, it is respectful and professional to pay them for their expertise and time. (After all, time spent supporting you and doing work that is academically rigorous for them as well is time away from their job, family, friends, and hobbies.) If you hire a mentor, always ask their rate ahead of time, including how they accept payment, and directly tell them what support you're looking for. That will help the potential mentor decide if their skills are a good match for your needs. Finally, if this is a route you're interested in, it's most beneficial to find a mentor *before* you start collecting data and writing. If you present a mentor with a nearly completed portfolio with a flawed premise, there isn't much they can do to help, save for telling you to start over ... which *they* won't want to tell you, and *you* won't want to hear!
- Work with a proofreader. Although you are not assessed on your language skills (including spelling, grammar, and punctuation), it does not hurt to put your best foot forward and have someone proofread your work.

If you are a non-native speaker of English, support is even more crucial, as the bulk of the portfolio writing is in English. In this case, it would be ideal to have support from an NBCT who shares the same native language, if possible. In addition, we recommend asking for the extra time accommodation on the Component 1 test, as the multiple choice questions are in English.

The moral of the story: Don't go it alone! Choose the right kind of support level for you, and lean on others.

Now that you have an idea of how and where the NBC process can fit into your life, the next step is to dig in and plan your portfolio!

2
Planning Your Portfolio

In the last chapter, we covered some "Calendar Talk." In other words, when is the best time to start the process? After you have your start year nailed down, it's time to take the next steps in the setup process. Don't skip these steps, as they build a foundation that supports success in each NBPTS component submission.

Set-Up

Once you know when you're going to officially register with the NBPTS and start a component, create an "ideal calendar" from *now* through submission of the component. This can be digital, sketched out in a notebook, or integrated into a planner, and it should include designated time (up to several hours per week) to think and plan in the months leading up to registration.

> Take time over the summer to read through all the directions and make a plan for how you might want to approach each part of the portfolio. [Doing] the conceptual legwork without having other course work to plan and grade is invaluable.
> —Megan Chvatal, NBCT since 2014

Next, it's time to gather supplies! Print out the NBPTS portfolio instructions *and* the rubric for the component you're starting with. Having these two documents side by side while armed with a highlighter, pen, and Post-It flags will help you stay organized and make it easier to note the parts you feel are the most important and that you might want to come back to.

Third, read all of the chapters in Section 1 of this book. These chapters are vital for persuasive submissions for Components 2–4. Skip these chapters to your detriment!

Finally, it's time to plan the specifics of the component you're working on. When candidates take the time to plan their entry *before* gathering the necessary evidence, we believe the chances of success go up considerably! Component 1 (Chapter 6) is a bit different because it's a one-day exam, but Components 2–4 (Chapters 7–9) can be planned months or even a year in advance. For this planning, we recommend four main steps:

> **Step 1:** After you have printed out the NBPTS portfolio instructions and the rubric for the component you're working on, *read them!* This book doesn't replace published instructions; it's a supplement. When you read through the guides from the NBPTS, mark them up! Highlight, underline, write notes, jot down questions ... anything you need to do to sort out what you need to accomplish.
>
> **Step 2:** Start reading the chapter of the component you're working on. Chapters 7–9 all begin with a summary of the component, an overview of what you'll turn in, a list of what we believe assessors are looking for, and a planning section, including a Your Turn! area to generate ideas. It is crucial to brainstorm ideas and possible routes you can take for each portfolio submission *before* you start gathering evidence. Why? It is not uncommon for candidates to generate *one* idea, gather evidence, see it through to the end, and feel like it wasn't the right choice ... but have no time left to

pivot and change course. Not only do they often not have time to change course, but if they never made Plan B or Plan C (or more!), they have nothing to fall back on. Furthermore, we all know that a plan can look *so good* on paper ... and then we add students into the mix and, somehow, the original brilliant idea doesn't *quite* go as planned. It can be wise to collect evidence for multiple classes, units, or students (depending on the component you're working on) over the course of a semester or more, and then consider which one best showcases your accomplished practice. This will also help you get better at collecting the sort of evidence the NBPTS is looking for.

Step 3: After you have generated ideas in the first Your Turn! section for your component, come back to this chapter to re-read the Important Factors to Consider sections. These factors are inextricably linked to a strong portfolio submission for Components 2–4. Do not skip them; instead, strive for ways to integrate them into your work. You may find it helpful to flag those sections so they're easy to refer back to.

Step 4: If you're hoping to work with a mentor, now is the time to set up your first meeting! The "sweet spot" for beginning work with a mentor is *after* you have planned a few (different) ideas and *before* you have narrowed down and implemented one idea. A good mentor will be able to walk through the ideas you have and help you choose the strongest path.

Important Established Factors to Consider

No matter which component you're working on, you should weave a few key elements throughout your submission. To continue with the weaving analogy, these key factors are the warp (vertical threads) of your submission, and your unique teaching is the weft (horizontal threads). Individually, they're just threads, but together, they make a strong fabric that can be cut, shaped, and sewn into something beautiful. The same is true for your Components 2–4 submissions; using the following information as a backbone to your own work will only strengthen it.

The 5 Core Propositions. These are directly from the NBPTS, and they form the basis of what the NBPTS believes constitutes accomplished teaching. In order:
- ◊ Proposition 1: Teachers are committed to students and their learning.
- ◊ Proposition 2: Teachers know the subjects they teach and how to teach those subjects to students.
- ◊ Proposition 3: Teachers are responsible for managing and monitoring student learning.
- ◊ Proposition 4: Teachers think systematically about their practice and learn from experience.
- ◊ Proposition 5: Teachers are members of learning communities.

Pay attention to these propositions! The NBPTS wants to know that each person to whom they confer a title of NBCT provides "clear, consistent, and convincing" evidence (their words) that they exemplify these propositions. You may also notice that the Core Propositions directly relate to the NBPTS scoring rubrics and to the components themselves. We feel the strongest ties lie here:
- ◊ Component 1: Proposition 2
- ◊ Component 2: Propositions 1, 2, 3, and 4
- ◊ Component 3: Propositions 1, 2, 3, and 4
- ◊ Component 4: Propositions 1, 4, and 5

We recommend printing out The 5 Core Propositions and having them posted next to the place where you work on your submissions. Continually refer back to them and let them guide your process ("Five Core Propositions," National Board for Professional Teaching Standards).

The Architecture of Accomplished Teaching. This also comes directly from the NBPTS. In fact, it is the guiding framework for what the NBPTS is trying to build in their

certified teachers; it is the practical application of the Core Propositions:
- ◊ 1st: Your Students: Who are they? Where are they now? What do they need, and in what order do they need it? Where should I begin? (This is related to Proposition 1.)
- ◊ 2nd: Set high, worthwhile goals appropriate for these students, at this time, in this setting. (Proposition 1)
- ◊ 3rd: Implement instruction designed to attain those goals. (Proposition 2)
- ◊ 4th: Evaluate student learning in light of the goals and the instruction. (Proposition 3)
- ◊ 5th: Reflect on student learning, the effectiveness of the instructional design, particular concerns, and issues. (Proposition 4)
- ◊ 6th: Set new high and worthwhile goals that are appropriate for these students at this time. (Proposition 3)

Like other documents, it may be beneficial to print the Architecture of Accomplished Teaching diagram from the NBPTS website and keep it in your workspace ("Architecture of Accomplished Teaching," National Board for Professional Teaching Standards).

American Council on the Teaching of Foreign Languages (ACTFL) proficiency levels. For all of the U.S., ACTFL is the "governing body" for world language education. It doesn't matter if you teach in a small school or large school, rural or urban, public or private; ACTFL is at the head of what we do, and their language proficiency levels set the basis for our work. We recommend being familiar enough with the ACTFL proficiency levels that you can integrate them into your writing and reflections. For example, the proficiency levels can easily be incorporated into the goals you set (and then write about) for your students. In the Component 1 constructed response questions, referencing the ACTFL proficiency levels can be an effective way to describe student achievement.

Standards. Knowledge of standards relates to the 5 Core Propositions and to the Architecture of Accomplished

Teaching. In short, knowing what standards you're striving to meet is part of a strong professional practice. The NBPTS does not mention including *specific* standards into your portfolio submissions; however, you should consider and integrate whichever standards are most appropriate to you, your students, your goals, and your overall context. These may be ACTFL standards, state standards, or even district standards. What's important is not the standard itself; the relevant piece is your knowledge of the standard and how you choose to reflect that knowledge in your classroom and pedagogical practice. Including one or two standards in your writing can demonstrate your professionalism.

Research. Much like the various standards we work with, including established research into your submissions isn't *required*, but it can be a way to show your professionalism and knowledge of best practices. *If* you choose to reference research, we recommend doing it in just a few short words; long quotes of research will take up valuable space and, most importantly, do nothing to showcase *your* practice. The assessors are all experienced world language teachers, and they will be familiar with the major research in our field.

Part of an accomplished practice is being knowledgeable about the work other people or entities have done that has major implications for our field. Staying up to date on current best practices will strengthen your submission and your classroom practice.

Important "Open" Factors to Consider

The 5 Core Propositions, the Architecture of Accomplished Teaching, ACTFL proficiency levels, various world language standards, and language acquisition research are all pre-established. In other words, another entity created them, and you have to figure out how they factor into your teaching and learning context. There are a couple more factors (in the form of questions) that are much more open and that we consider to be key components to planning a successful portfolio submission:

Should I Take a Risk or Play It Safe? This is a frequently asked question by candidates working on Components 2 and 3 in particular. It's a fair question and one you should take into account early in the planning phase. The short answer is, "Risk it!" But why?

First, remember that the NBCT distinction is considered the gold standard in teacher certification. In other words, this is where you should showcase your best teaching; this is no place for an "everyday" strategy or lesson. For example, it's fair to say that at some point in our world language classes, we all do some form of choral responses to practice pronunciation. But let's be clear: Choral responses aren't rocket science. It's not a difficult strategy, nor does it require skilled planning or higher-order thinking from the students or teacher. Therefore, featuring this or a similar strategy does little to prove you are an accomplished practitioner.

It is our strong opinion that the NBC process is an excellent place to try something innovative and/or new! Playing it 100% safe in teaching is not a 100% safe strategy in NBC. You may worry, "But what if I don't meet my goals?" We argue that it's actually *okay* not to meet all of your goals as long as you're appropriately reflecting and coming up with a *"Because of* the result, I'm doing *this* next" plan. A creative idea to solve a problem that doesn't go perfectly gives you more to write about and is more interesting than picking a simple goal that you accomplish every year. It's also worth considering that your assessor will be reading *many* entries. If they read yours, and it's full of strategies that *every* teacher does in nearly *every* unit, it's a heavier lift to try to convince them that you have intentionally designed the instruction for this particular context. On the other hand, if you can present something innovative or unique, this demonstrates your accomplished teaching and shows that you are looking for solutions to these students' problems. You want your assessor to think, "Wow, that's brilliant! I want to try that in my classroom!"

We hope the "Start planning early!" message is beginning to sound like a broken record. Yet another reason why it's wise to do so is because if you try something new and innovative, and it doesn't go well *at all*, it's not a problem! Scrap it! Do something different! If you've planned in advance and have a variety of ideas to choose from, you will feel much less stress when something doesn't go according to plan because you will have given yourself the gift of time.

> If you are not happy with any part of your work, redo it.
> It's part of the process.
> —Thomas Soth, NBCT since 2006

How do I integrate the target culture(s)? Integrating one or more target cultures into your portfolio submission isn't just good for the submission; it's good for kids, and it's best practice.

First, consider how you can use authentic resources. (We recognize that there is a debate in the world language world about what, exactly, constitutes an "authentic resource." For the purposes of this book, it doesn't matter if you consider authentic resources to be limited to resources created by native speakers for real-world purposes, or if your view allows for a broader range of acceptable resources. Rather, what matters is that you understand the resources and can convincingly explain why a particular resource is "authentic" to you.) In order to find resources, consider where you can source them for free. State or national organizations for your target language can be invaluable in this pursuit! Another helpful resource can be target language teacher groups on social media platforms. Post a question (e.g., "I'm looking for resources for ____. Does anyone know of a good one?" or "I'm looking for ways to integrate X, an authentic resource from ____, into a lesson. Does anyone have ideas for me?") and, likely, you'll have a slew of responses from other teachers across the country. There's no need to operate solo; lean on other teachers for help finding what you need, and then (importantly!) make it your own.

Second, examine how you can integrate ACTFL's three P's of culture: products, practices, and/or perspectives. Products are things a target culture has created, physical or non-physical. Practices are typical behaviors, interactions, and expectations for what to do in a given situation. Perspectives encompass attitudes, values, and beliefs that are often the undercurrent driving both products and practices. This is another viable area for throwing out calls for ideas to colleagues across the country via social media!

Third, recognize the potential for using more than one target culture. You may have a creative idea for including multiple target cultures into a single lesson, and that's wonderful! But another approach is spreading out knowledge of different cultures among the components (e.g., focusing on Mexico in Component 2, but branching into Panama and Colombia in Component 3). Additionally, don't neglect how ACTFL's "5 C" goal areas (Communication, Cultures, Connections, Comparisons, Communities) could be used here. For example, take "Comparisons": Could you build that into a lesson that integrates multiple cultures? Finally, be mindful not to default to any one culture. This tends to be a more common issue among French teachers; France and the French tend to be the default culture, but incorporating a broader and more accurate representation of "la francophonie" is a wonderful way to demonstrate your accomplished practice.

While we don't see the NBPTS *requiring* teachers to take a risk, use authentic resources, highlight more than one target culture, and include products, practices, and perspectives anywhere in their guides, we do think these additions to your work showcase your knowledge of best practices in world language instruction and can bolster a powerful submission.

It may not be neat and tidy or look "perfect" (so boring...) yet, but if you followed the steps from this chapter, spent time reflecting, and have been planning your first component –

timelines, possibilities, lists of what you may want to add, printouts of the concepts you want to guide your work – you have an excellent start, and you're on the right track! Successful portfolios tightly weave these pedagogies and practices throughout their submissions, creating a snazzy tapestry of accomplished teaching from beginning to end. (Middle school teachers, we see you. We already know that tapestry isn't going on the wall. You're fastening it around your neck and transforming yourself into a superhero for class today. Time to go save students from ho-hum instruction!)

Next up: examining how to write for Components 2–4. (Spoiler alert: It's different from most writing you do.)

References

"Architecture of Accomplished Teaching." *National Board for Professional Teaching Standards*. NBPTS, 2024, www.nbpts.org/. Accessed 7 Aug. 2025.

"Five Core Propositions." *National Board for Professional Teaching Standards*, First published 1989; updated 2016, *What Teachers Should Know and Be Able to Do*, NBPTS, 2025, www.nbpts.org/certification/five-core-propositions/. Accessed 7 Aug. 2025.

3

A Specific Kind of Writing

This is a bit of a Choose Your Own Adventure chapter! Do you want the short version of how to write for the NBPTS portfolio or the long version? It's up to you!

The Short Version

The entirety of the NBPTS portfolio requires you to write in a specific way. The essential piece to remember is that you're not writing for an English class. In other words, the portfolio writing isn't *artistic*; it's more *scientific*. Think of it like writing a lab report for what goes on in your classroom. Most of what we do linguistically in our daily lives is describing and planning, but this writing is focused on *analyzing*. The rhythm you will follow is: Read the question. Give an answer. Provide evidence. Repeat.

That's it! On paper, it's simple! However, we have learned through mentoring candidates that not everyone's brain works that way. (And that's okay!) So if you feel like you need more tips, explanations, and a more thorough breakdown of the writing style and how to successfully implement it, read on!

The Long Version

Let's start small and move toward more robust writing strategies and tips.

What we believe the assessors are looking for: The NBPTS documents assert that they are looking for *clear, consistent, and convincing evidence* that you meet the standards in the portfolio rubrics. As you answer each question in the portfolio documents, ask yourself:

> Is this clear ... or am I muddying up my main point?
>
> Am I consistent in my approach ... or am I all over the place?
>
> Is the point I'm trying to make convincing ... or is the evidence I'm providing too weak?

Successful portfolios maintain this standard throughout the submission.

Instructional Context: For Components 2–4 (C2–C4), most candidates begin their written work by filling out the one-page forms, such as the Instructional Context sheets. When we mentor candidates, this is the first thing we read, as it provides the necessary background for what happens in the classroom, and it's safe to assume assessors do the same. It's difficult to understand the Instructional Planning form (C3) and the Written Commentaries (C2–C4), for example, if you don't have a clear picture of who is in the classroom and what life is like at the school.

In the Instructional Context sheets (C2–C4), include items that impact your daily life as a teacher. You may want to consider: wifi stability, number of preps/levels you teach, bi/multilingualism in the classroom, level of parent involvement, attendance rates, literacy rates in the dominant language of the school, resources, technology availability, IEPs and 504 plans in the classroom, identified gifted students, and shared space, among others. These are one-page snapshots of your classroom, and if you feel like you don't have enough space, you're writing too much. There is nothing you need to *explain* or *describe* in a narrative manner here; rather, you're writing short sentences that are to the point. Keep it simple, and include what is necessary for your assessors to understand.

What the assessors already know: Your NBPTS scorers are professional world language teachers, current or retired. This works to your advantage! Because your assessor is or was a world language teacher, some points are *known entities*, and you don't have to describe them. What does that mean? Let's say you work in an International Baccalaureate school. After you write, "I work in an International Baccalaureate (IB) high school," there is no need to explain what International Baccalaureate *means*; assume the assessors know because International Baccalaureate is global. Here's another example: If you write, "My department exclusively uses Comprehensible Input (CI) strategies in language acquisition classes," there is no need to explain what Comprehensible Input is. The same is true for defining other well-known educational terms, such as Advanced Placement, concurrent enrollment, popcorn reading, or a jigsaw activity. Experienced educators are familiar with these (and similar) terms. Conversely, if a program is unique to your school or district, that may require a short description. In that case, a candidate may say something like, "I supervise the Ambassadors program (student leadership group) at my school." In that situation, the Ambassadors program is unique to the school, but there is no need to say everything that the group does; a simple, yet accurate parenthetical phrase will do the trick.

Space: As candidates work through their component submissions, it is common to lament, "There isn't enough space! I'm supposed to write four pages, but I'm currently on page 20, and I'm not even done!" Now, that's an exaggeration … but it's not far off, in our experience! Always bear in mind the following: You absolutely have enough space. If you feel like you don't, you're not being clear enough and need to re-work your approach to the questions.

The extent to which you write over the required page count will give some clues into what your mistakes are. Let's say your writing exceeds a 4-page requirement by half a page or even a full page. Likely, you simply need to edit. The (sometimes painful) editing process refines writing and increases clarity. When candidates we mentor go over the word count, it makes their work *less* clear instead of *more* clear.

For candidates whose page counts are grossly over the limit, it's typically more than a simple editing issue, although that likely still plays a role. In these situations, it is extremely common for the candidate to have *described* instead of *analyzed*. You don't need to give a play-by-play of everything that happened; instead, briefly mention the situation that occurred and spend your time (and space) analyzing what it showed you, what you did in response, and why. In brief, always directly answer the prompt or question presented in the NBPTS guide. Weak portfolios tend to cover questions that weren't asked (e.g., describing) or that only loosely relate to the question. Another possibility, however, for documents going grossly over the page count is simply not following the format and word choice suggestions that follow.

It is typical for candidates to try to fix the problem of going over the page count by using every shorthand imaginable (e.g., changing all instances of "and" to "&," changing all instances of "students" to "Ss") throughout their portfolio. You should always refer to the NBPTS guides for what's allowed and what's not, but after you determine that, we advise using as few shorthands as possible. To be clear, using acronyms (e.g., ACTFL, AP, IB) is not the same as using shorthand (e.g., &, Ss). Common acronyms, as long as you have previously defined them, are easy to read and don't appear as often in the portfolio. On the other hand, including too many shorthand notations can quickly make your writing confusing and difficult to read, which then impedes clarity. One final note about shorthands: Be especially wary of shorthands that are not *standard* but are *texting lingo,* such as "ur" instead of "your" or "you're" or omitting apostrophes entirely. This is unprofessional and should be completely avoided.

While most candidates with space issues are experiencing the problem of going *over* the maximum page count, going significantly under the page count is also possible, though far less frequent. If you have a lot of space left or are struggling to fill space, it's time to revisit the questions. Ask yourself if you're being clear, consistent, and convincing ... and, most importantly, did you answer every part of the prompts? Then ask a mentor or colleague to read what you wrote, and verify with *them* if it's clear, consistent, and convincing. If they report that it's not, ask what would make it better.

> I found it extremely helpful to have an experienced [NBCT] person read my writing. I started all my answers with the question stem, but a colleague helped me see that in a number of cases, I was nonetheless not truly [homing] in on the aspects they wanted us to address. A practiced eye can help you see if you are on the right path!
> —French teacher, NBCT since 2021

Format: As previously stated, the format of writing for the NBPTS portfolio is quite simple: Read the question. Give an answer. Provide evidence. Repeat.

When working within that format, there are important points to consider. First, it is critical to remain *laser focused*. For Components 2–4, everything you should do (and, therefore, everything you should write about) has to be intentional: specific for *this* student or class and for *this* pedagogical situation. It is common for candidates to simply go too broad in their writing, which is a considerable mistake.

Remember that this writing is akin to writing a lab report in science. You're stating the facts and providing evidence; you're not writing an essay for an English class. You need neither an opening thesis nor a conclusion. There are a variety of ways you can train yourself to stick to this style, including helpful transition phrases and structures such as:

- I did X because…
- I think my student…because…so I did X.
- For example…
- I noticed…, so I did X.
- My student said or wrote X. This showed me…
- When X happened, I realized … because…
- I initially planned to … but because of X, I did Y instead.
- I anticipated (or didn't anticipate) X, so I decided to Y, because…

When candidates employ these structures, it creates clear language that follows a consistent pattern: I know my content and my students, so I ___. In other words, you're succinctly showing your professionalism, intentionality, and strength as an educator!

A second point to acknowledge is the structure of your submission document as a whole. Let's use C3 as an example. As of this publication, the Written Commentary for C3 can be no more than four pages, and within that, there are seven bullet points the NBPTS wants candidates to address. Separate your answers for each bullet point and keep them in the same order as they appear in the NBPTS component guide. This helps the assessor know where your answers are, which, in turn, makes it easier to score.

Third, as you're following the flow of the questions in the NBPTS guide, take note of the key words. For example, if a prompt/question asks about your goal(s) for the unit, your answer should include the word "goal." This is a simple technique to help your submission be more clear and easier to follow for the assessor.

Fourth, pay attention to how many parts the prompt has, as many prompts have multiple parts. Candidates frequently write extensively (and often overly so) about one part of the prompt and do not address a subsequent part adequately or at all. Watch out: This can be as simple as responding to two *different sentences* within the same bullet point in the component guide OR it can be as subtle as identifying and responding to the first and second parts *of a single sentence*. Failing to adequately respond to all parts of the prompts can be especially common when there's a prompt including something we might regularly use in our own daily practice, followed by another part of the question we don't ask ourselves as often, leading to neglect. Look for examples of this type of error in the Case Study segments in this book.

Word choice: There is no need for flowery, poetic, or creative language use in the C2–4 portfolio submissions, and it's important to be clear, consistent, and convincing. But what else is notable for word choice?

Unfortunately, a common issue in portfolio writing is filling it with "word salad." There is no need for your portfolio to look like an educational jargon dictionary just took over your submissions in a take-no-prisoners-style attack! Worse, word salad often underscores a bigger problem: the submission is not strong enough.

Word salad typically surrounds a less-than-convincing answer to a question. In Chapter 2, we tackled the essential question, "Should I take a risk or play it safe?" (To reiterate, we stand firm that taking a risk is the better choice.) We discussed "everyday" types of activities that many teachers do but that aren't suitable for starring roles in the portfolio, such as choral pronunciation practice. Other equally uninspired activities may include completing grammar worksheets or making vocabulary flashcards. A candidate practicing a word salad strategy may, for example, write extensively about filling in a grammar worksheet and litter the paragraph with an abundance of words like *differentiation, scaffolding, spiraling the curriculum, Bloom's Taxonomy, backwards design,* and *comprehensible input*. It's hard to read this type of submission without envisioning an old, grizzled grandfather sitting in a rocking chair on a porch, shaking his head and saying in a gruff voice, "You can't polish a turd, son"… and he wouldn't be wrong! You simply can't fix an inherently flawed submission, no matter how fancy you attempt to make it sound with educational jargon. The assessors will absolutely know you're trying to use those words to cover up a lackluster submission.

Reflection: Arguably, the most vital piece of the C2–C4 submissions is the reflections that appear in the Written Commentary sections. This includes answering questions about what you might do differently next time and what next steps you will take as a result of what happened in your classroom.

In our mentoring experience, it is typical for candidates to answer in one of two extremes: 1. Everything went perfectly, or 2. Everything went wrong. In a creative, pedagogically-sound, and well-planned lesson, it is highly likely that neither is accurate.

As mentioned in Chapter 2, if everything *truly* did go wrong and if you gave yourself plenty of time, scrap your lesson and try something new. You'll feel better about it if you do! Then, when you achieve a lesson (or, depending on the component, an assessment, etc.) you're *mostly* content with, we recommend following this pattern:

Say the lesson was great *and why*.

State what could make it even better next time *and why*.

Outline the next steps for these students *and why*.

Following this structure proves you know your content *and* your students, which is a primary goal of your portfolio submission as a whole because it follows the Architecture of Accomplished Teaching (Chapter 2) set forth by the NBPTS.

We advise candidates to bear in mind that assessors probably aren't looking for a perfect lesson, if there is such a thing. They are, however, looking for a *strong* lesson that includes evidence that you used data and best practices to plan, made adjustments in real time to meet students' needs, accurately analyzed your own effectiveness, and planned for the future based on what you learned. Where are they going to find this evidence? In your clear, consistent, and convincing writing. Remember: Read the question. Give an answer. Provide evidence. Repeat.

4

Bookends

Knowledge of Students and Reflection

Components 2–4 (C2–4) have strong structural similarities. Among them is the fact that knowledge of students plays a significant *opening* role in the work, and your ability to think critically and reflect before, during, and after the work is done is the *closing* step. Think of your knowledge of students and your reflection as bookends to these component portfolio entries.

Opening Bookend: Knowledge of Students

How do we know that demonstrating knowledge of students is vital to your submissions? It's right there in step 1 of the Architecture of Accomplished Teaching:

> Your Students: Who are they? Where are they now? What do they need and in what order do they need it? Where should I begin?
> ("Architecture of Accomplished Teaching," National Board for Professional Teaching Standards)

Knowledge of students is essential in every NBC component, and wise candidates remember that this knowledge

DOI: 10.4324/9781003716860-5

is multifaceted. First, it's knowing about students *in general*, including content such as (but not limited to) how students learn, how they acquire language, what works well, and what doesn't work well for different kinds of learners. This information, in particular, presents itself most overtly in C1. Second, it's knowing about *your own students* with content like (but not limited to) who they are, how they show up in your classroom, what makes them tick, what (if any) second language experiences they've had, and where their talents, interests, and struggles lie. This second type of knowledge of students is most prevalent in C2–C4, and it's our focus in the first part of this chapter.

Knowledge of students can be gathered in a qualitative or quantitative fashion, and neither is superior. Ultimately, it's entirely dependent on your specific context and your portfolio submission plan, as different types of knowledge will support different instructional plans. The following lists are designed to help you consider different sources from which you can draw to demonstrate knowledge of students, though the lists are by no means exhaustive. We recommend circling any you feel are particularly pertinent to the portfolio submission you're currently building. Alternatively, use three different colors of highlighters (one each for C2–C4) and highlight which sources might be most applicable to that component's requirements and your approach to the submission.

Examples of assessment or school-based data:

- Standardized test scores
- GPA or grades
- Students' current or past course enrollment (e.g., AP or IB classes, common electives, prior language study experiences). Note: Prior language experiences are specified in the C2 rubric, so they need to be included with that component.
- Students' previous performance in a world language
- Assessments from your classes, other classes, or from prior years of study
- Demographic information

- Special needs (e.g., IEPs, 504s, exceptionality, health concerns)
- Language proficiency levels (in your target language or in other languages; broken down by skill or as a composite score)
- School-wide, composite information about students' living situations, such as socioeconomic status, access to technology, home language(s), and caregiver support. (Or info specific to your students, if you can get that from a school-based data system.)
- My idea: _____

Examples of observational data:

- Notes, comments, or quotes from previous years' world language teachers
- Your own classroom observations. It's great if you can quantify this with phrases like "# students did X during this activity."
- Student comments during class. Jot these down for use in your writing.
- Data, testimonials, or other information from school-based professionals (e.g., counselors, other teachers, coaches, special education teachers, health care providers, specialists such as the ESL teacher, the IB coordinator, the Career Development Director)
- My idea: _____

Examples of information from parents and caregivers:

- Parent conferences, in-person meetings, conversations
- Parent surveys. This is a helpful tool, but you can only realistically send parent surveys sparingly, so take time to develop your survey questions thoughtfully. One approach is to send a parent survey as you are narrowing down your goals for the component; then you can ask questions related to those goals to use in your entry.

Consider giving parents some closed-ended questions (e.g., rate from 1 to 5, agree or disagree) and one or two open-ended questions; this structure gives you both statistics and (hopefully) good parent quotes.
- My idea: _____

Examples of information directly from students:

- Information students share regarding their own living situations, such as socioeconomic status, access to technology, home language, travel experiences, and caregiver support
- Student interest or "get to know you" questionnaires, including questions about hobbies, extracurriculars, interests, other classes, college and/or career goals, language goals, reasons for taking the class, and past experiences with world language study, among others
- Student assignments
- Student reflections on their work
- Course evaluations or feedback forms
- Prior assessments in your class, either formative or summative
- Exit tickets
- My idea: _____

Examples of community characteristics:

- Demographics, socioeconomic information
- Major employers
- Local events that impact students
- Availability of infrastructure, transportation, technology, amenities
- Feeder schools or schools your students will feed into
- Unique characteristics of your school
- Unique characteristics of your community that may influence community and/or school identity and output
- My idea: _____

Now that you've collected data to demonstrate your knowledge of students, combine it with your knowledge of language acquisition to curate appropriate goals for these students at this moment. Look for data points that all illustrate the same student need; this need will determine your unit goals. The goals you select will drive the rest of your entry (C2–C4), so it's vital they're tightly aligned to your knowledge of students. Failure to clearly demonstrate how knowledge of students directly influenced the choice of goals is one of the most significant errors a candidate can make.

Your Turn!

While working on C2-C4, come back to these questions to brainstorm and plan how you will integrate your knowledge of students into your portfolio submission.

Possible data source to demonstrate knowledge of students:

How I know this/How I will gather this data:

What I learned about my student(s) from this data:

How this knowledge influenced my planning and instruction/ How I customized goals and instruction for these students because of this data:

Common Pitfalls for Demonstrating Knowledge of Students

There are only a few frequent pitfalls for proving knowledge of students, but they are significant because they are the foundation of accomplished practice:

- Listing a lot of disjointed information that doesn't correspond to students' needs
- Glossing over knowledge of students with too few sources/data points
- Failing to use your knowledge of students to drive unit goals

Having a deep knowledge of students is the basis for each of your C2–C4 portfolio entries, in which you must demonstrate that you customized your instruction for *these* students based on *this* knowledge. We believe a casual approach to establishing knowledge of students has been many candidates' downfall.

Closing Bookend: Reflection

How do we know that strong reflection is critical to your success? As with the opening bookend "Knowledge of Students," "Reflection" is right there in the Architecture of Accomplished Teaching, steps 5 and 6:

> Reflect on student learning, the effectiveness of the instructional design, particular concerns, and issues.
>
> Set new high and worthwhile goals that are appropriate for <u>these students</u> at <u>this time</u>.

Reflection, in particular, is the heart of one of the NBPTS 5 Core Propositions as well:

> Teachers think systematically about their practice and learn from experience.
>
> ("Five Core Propositions," National Board for Professional Teaching Standards)

Each of the Written Components requires candidates to reflect on their work. Reflection is one of the NBPTS standards, and it is based on the belief that "For accomplished teachers, every classroom experience provides an opportunity for reflection and improvement" ("World Language Standards," National Board for Professional Teaching Standards, 43). This does not mean you should be overly critical or negative about your lessons! You want to show that your instruction was successful overall, due to your accomplished practice. An effective reflection conveys, "This lesson was great! Here's why: _____. And I have a couple of ideas to make it even better next time."

The NBPTS World Language Standards indicate accomplished practitioners embrace these qualities in their reflection:

- A focus on meeting student needs
- Analyzing successes
- Analyzing setbacks
- Rethinking instructional choices
- Openness to innovation
- Continually seeking "information, assistance, and ideas"
- Creativity
- Personal Growth
- Staying current in educational research and trends
- Staying current with technology
- Consistent evaluation of the impact of their own actions in the classroom and student achievement

Your reflection should focus on how your accomplished instruction resulted in positive student outcomes, how you know, and what you will do next time to ensure your students continue to thrive.

Common Pitfalls in the Reflection Section

As you reflect on your practice, avoid these errors:

- Describing instead of analyzing. At this point, your assessors have already read most of your entry, so you can mention examples briefly and get to the analysis.

Use phrases like "I realized...", "This showed me...", "Because..." to illustrate your thinking concerning classroom events. If you allot too much space simply to *describing* what happened, your assessors may conclude your entry lacks evidence of reflective practice.
- Emphasizing the negative. Show your lesson was effective, and you know why. Mention one or two possible adjustments with an emphasis on making it even better than it already was!
- Shallow points for improvement. Logistical changes or minor tweaks to content will not convince assessors of your accomplished reflection. Look for areas that are related to improving the quality of students' learning experience (e.g., a way to improve students' background knowledge or a requisite skill, a place where you could integrate more cultural knowledge or an additional communication mode, a reason to change your sequencing, a place to incorporate another resource or collaboration).

The ability to reflect on the work we've done, determine adjustments to better serve our students, and move forward despite any (perceived) failures we encountered is pivotal to success, not just in NBC but in our everyday classroom lives. So be honest, be positive, and keep progress at the forefront of your work.

Case Study Practice

Using the guidance in this chapter, what significant errors did each of these teachers make?

Example 1: Ms. Murdoch thought it wise to tie her reflection back to her original goals: Improve students' feelings of safety in class. Increase the percentage of students who move on to the next level of Spanish. Increase students' ability to correctly differentiate between *por* and *para*.

Increase the length of time students can successfully hold a conversation in Spanish with a partner. Decrease the amount of wait time she gives before students settle down, and she can begin the lesson.
Ms. Murdoch's Error:

Example 2: Mr. Feeny liked his lesson and thought it went well, but he wasn't sure what assessors would think, and he wanted to show that he can do even better. In his reflection, he highlighted five significant errors he felt should be improved. He analyzed why they were problems and what his next steps were because of these problems.
Mr. Feeny's Error:

Example 3: Mr. Rooney collected student data from eleven different sources. He used 8 point font and .25-inch margins in order to fit all the data in the allotted space. In his class profile, he listed detailed statistics about the students' demographics, academic performance, and home lives. Since his students are in level 3, he chose the objective of mastering object pronouns as his unit focus.
Mr. Rooney's Error:

Example 4: Mr. Garrison expertly detailed his lesson in his reflection, starting with what he did to prepare, continuing with each step of the lesson (including in-the-moment pivots he had to make based on what happened in class), and finishing with the class wrap-up. He was positive that there would be no margin for error and that his assessors would see exactly how the class went down that day.
Mr. Garrison's Error:

Example 5: Ms. Johnson was eager to show assessors her excellent lesson design. After noting a couple of facts about her students' GPAs and demographics, she jumped right into the real part of her Written Commentary.
Ms. Johnson's Error:

 Case Study Analysis

Let's examine each teacher's error.

Example 1: Ms. Murdoch may certainly want and/or need to accomplish those goals to have a more successful classroom. However, she chose too many goals, they're loosely (if at all) related, and she needs to show why the (appropriate, related) goals she chose were appropriate for *these* students at *this* time based on *specific* data.

Example 2: It's okay that Mr. Feeny had elements of his lesson he wanted to improve, but he didn't accentuate the positive. If it was, in fact, a solid lesson, it would have been better for him to say it was successful, analyze why/how, and justify one or two tweaks to make it even better next time.

Example 3: While Mr. Rooney has collected a lot of data, he hasn't demonstrated how he prioritizes or uses this data to draw thoughtful conclusions about his students' needs. In fact, the goal Mr. Rooney has selected doesn't seem to have any connection to this particular class at all, but rather is part of a predetermined curricular sequence. Mr. Rooney needs to prioritize the data he collected to identify appropriate goals for this group of students.

Example 4: The reflection doesn't call for *description*; it calls for *analysis*. Mr. Garrison spent too much time describing and neglected to analyze what the results of his lesson showed, how he knew that, and based on that data, what his plans are for the subsequent lesson and/or for the next time he teaches this same lesson.

Example 5: Ms. Johnson did not show convincing knowledge of students through data points connected to her goal(s). Failing to see this as an important piece of the puzzle, she skipped ahead to the Written Commentary. She needs to show how her knowledge of students drove her choice of goals and subsequent instruction.

Bookending submissions by first demonstrating strong knowledge of your students and finally by conducting deep, meaningful, and analytical reflection is one of the best ways to prove your accomplished practice. These concepts are intimately linked to the Architecture of Accomplished Teaching and to the Five Core Propositions and, therefore, to the rubrics the NBPTS assessors use to score your submissions. Now carry on and bookend strong!

References

"Architecture of Accomplished Teaching." *National Board for Professional Teaching Standards*. NBPTS, 2024, www.nbpts.org/. Accessed 7 Aug. 2025.

"Five Core Propositions." *National Board for Professional Teaching Standards*, First published 1989; updated 2016, *What Teachers Should Know and Be Able to Do*, NBPTS, 2025, www.nbpts.org/certification/five-core-propositions/. Accessed 7 Aug. 2025.

National Board for Professional Teaching Standards. *World Languages Standards: Second Edition for Teachers of Students Ages 3–18+*. Preface revised and reformatted 2015–16; originally published 2010. National Board for Professional Teaching Standards, 2010. www.nbpts.org/wp-content/uploads/2017/07/ECYA-WL.pdf. Accessed 7 Aug. 2025.

5
Common Overall Pitfalls

Throughout our years working with NBCT candidates in different capacities, a variety of issues show up time and again. Many of these pitfalls work their way throughout the other chapters in this book as well, and certainly in the chapters specifically focusing on Components 1–4 (C1–4), so you may wonder why we chose to include a full *chapter* on overall pitfalls. Fair question! And we have an easy answer: We understand there are some candidates who will skip right to the C1–4 chapters and disregard the rest of the book. (It's a gamble to spend that much money on the certification process and *not* do everything you can to prepare a solid submission, but hey, you do you, Chapter Skipping Wonders!) Conversely, there are other candidates who will read every word, underline, highlight, and flag sections that resonate with them. Ultimately, we are teachers, and just like in the classroom, we are trying to relay some of the most important information here, there, and everywhere so that our "students" (readers) have an opportunity to hear the message in multiple ways and, with any luck, remember it and successfully implement it in their work.

Generally, the most common pitfalls lie in five categories: planning-related, prompt-related, writing-related, specificity-related (a subcategory to the writing issue), and pitfalls related to finishing strong.

Planning-Related Pitfalls

First and foremost, we have seen far too many candidates not understand that the NBC process is *not* hoop jumping. It's not a "Submit these component requirements, and NBCT status will be bestowed upon you" type of situation. The work needs to be done *well* and in a clear, consistent, and convincing manner. Anyone who fails to plan for this fact is setting themselves up for a harder road than necessary.

Another problem we consistently see is not planning in advance. For most people, a general rule is to plan out your C2–4 entries at least a semester in advance. (If you remember from Chapter 2, this is also the perfect time to get a mentor, if that route is appropriate for you, because the mentor can give you feedback on your plan.) Proper time devoted to planning can solve other problems down the road.

One of the first things you'll do during the planning process is consider your goals for the task at hand. Individual component requirements vary, but it is easy for candidates to fall into one or more of these goal-related pitfalls: not connecting your goals to your student data, having too many goals, and changing/adding goals as you write. Attacking 2–3 specific goals (for these students, at this time) with purposeful intent can contribute to your success in creating a clear, consistent submission.

Part of planning is figuring out exactly what you're going to do, curriculum-wise, with your students. We highly recommend avoiding canned curriculum or curriculum you haven't intentionally curated. This isn't the time to snag a last-minute activity off the internet or from a colleague, nor is it time to fall back on a standard, unoriginal lesson. Instead, select authentic, culturally-rich resources *and* adapt whatever is necessary to support these students' target language development. This may include scaffolding the resources, creating related activities, and/or designing proficiency-based tasks. Your component submissions should represent your *very best teaching*. Full stop. And what does your very best teaching need? Ample time to plan.

Prompt-Related Pitfalls

Overthinking the questions is an error, though we understand that for some chronic overthinkers (in life!), this may be unavoidable at the outset. We're here to give you permission to stop and to take the prompts at face value. If you find yourself constantly thinking, "But do they actually mean…?" or "What if they are saying…?" or "Could that mean X…or Y…or Z…?" you're overthinking the prompts. Consequently, you will ramble in your writing, failing to be clear, consistent, and convincing. The prompts, truly, are straightforward and should be answered precisely. A logical place to practice this is in the Instructional Context forms. There, candidates should avoid a narrative and stick to the facts of the question. Use that same skill when answering the prompts in the other forms. For example, if a prompt asks for the length of your featured instructional sequence, you can answer in one sentence: *This instructional sequence (Unit 3) generally lasts four weeks.* Here, there is no need to give any sort of background information; it's a simple question with a simple answer.

Often, when candidates overthink a prompt, they end up not directly *answering* the prompt because they're trying to hit all the possible "what ifs." Not directly answering the prompt can also happen because of failure to read and respond to all parts of the prompt. For example, if the prompt asks, "How was student feedback provided and what was your rationale for providing it in this manner?" that's a two-part prompt. Candidates will often respond to the first part and miss the second part entirely. Since the two clauses are listed together in the same prompt, it's perfectly appropriate to put them together in the same paragraph to capitalize on space. It's wise to note that in many two-part prompts, the first part requires a description (short), and the second requires analysis (longer). Overlooking the second part of the prompt may lead to a lack of adequate analysis in your entry.

Writing-Related Pitfalls

Skipping around while detailing your lesson is a common pitfall. In order to keep a consistent and orderly flow to your writing, it is helpful to generally write chronologically, from the beginning to the end of your lesson. Although you may have all the necessary content there, not using a logical flow can make it difficult to follow.

Next, if you find yourself in the pitfall of rambling to fill space, it means one or more of the following: 1. You need to go into more depth, 2. You didn't answer every part of each prompt, and/or 3. You're tired. If the reason is because of #1 or #2, take a closer look at each prompt and compare what you wrote to the rubric. Likely, you'll find something you missed or didn't completely answer. But if the reason is because of #3, it's time to walk away and come back when you're feeling fresh.

Candidates can easily fall into the pitfall of not understanding when to describe versus when to analyze. To be clear, *both* are necessary. Let's start with a tip: Go through your draft, highlighting descriptions in one color and analysis in another. Then compare. There should be more analysis than description. You should explain the path from *data* to *informed action* to *what the results mean and why*.

Related to analysis, another pitfall is failing to explicitly state simple pedagogical choices that have become second nature. Strong teachers take many actions in the classroom intuitively (e.g., managing physical space, providing equitable access to resources, monitoring student comprehension and engagement, scaffolding instruction, differentiating, informally assessing during instruction). While the rationale for these actions may be evident to you, assessors cannot read your mind! If you make a simple pedagogical choice, *say so* in your commentary. State your thinking, even if it seems very obvious to you.

Specificity-Related Pitfalls

Failing to be specific in your writing can be a serious pitfall. When candidates are too general, they lack both the *how* and the *why* in their answers. When you consider the prompts, the related rubrics, the Five Core Propositions, and the Architecture of Accomplished Teaching, it's clear the NBPTS is looking for why you planned *this* content for *these* students at *this* moment in time. Let's look at some examples of steering your writing toward greater specificity for your responses:

- Phrasing: Instead of using general phrases such as "Many students…," be more specific with "X number of students…" Instead of stating "They did better," strengthen the assertion with "On the pretest, here was the stat:_____. On the post-test, here was the much better stat: _____."
- Sources: Instead of providing only one criterion for your actions, consider punching that up with two or three, especially if they're from different kinds of sources. For example, to demonstrate Knowledge of Students, in lieu of only using test scores and GPA, include more personal information about who the students are as people. When writing about planning, use more than students' hobbies to justify your ideas.
- Hard data: Quantitative and/or qualitative data that backs up your plan is incredibly powerful. This can include numeric statistics about your student(s), class, school, or community, or it could take the form of student or parent quotes, for example. Both types of data can be extremely compelling in supporting your work.

Finishing Strong Pitfalls

It's important to plan in advance to allow ample time for redos (if necessary) *and* time for proofreading for finishing touches. This includes checking your spelling, grammar, and punctuation, of course, as well as verifying that you have responded to all parts of the prompts in a direct manner.

Another finishing touch is evaluating your writing against the NBPTS rubrics. They provide rubrics for a reason—so candidates will see exactly how they will be scored—and it's a sizable error not to print out the rubrics and go through your submission with a fine-toothed comb, analyzing how it measures up. After you finish your strongest submission draft, we recommend waiting at least a few days before doing this rubric evaluation. Waiting will help you see your work more objectively.

Speaking of seeing objectively, if you've dug into this process at all before opening this book (e.g., reading the NBPTS guides or starting the actual portfolio submissions), you know how positively dizzying this can be! The work is *intense!* Because of this, many portfolios unravel toward the end. (You're tired! We know! We were too!) At this point, candidates may stop answering questions fully and begin making mistakes, like giving generalizations and rambling. Our best advice here is to *stop* when you notice yourself slipping; *stop* when you notice yourself saying, "I don't even know what I'm writing anymore." After you stop, *walk away!* Give yourself a break of multiple hours or days. When you come back fresh, it will be reflected in your work.

Unraveling at the end of a submission is commonplace, but sometimes it goes a step further: Some candidates become so burned out or discouraged that they want to quit. *We get it*, and if this is you at any point, you're not alone. This feeling can happen for a variety of reasons. Some candidates have a major life change while working on certification, or maybe they took on too much. Others might realize NBC is actually more time-intensive than they thought, or they might have a particularly challenging class and be questioning everything they thought they knew and felt about teaching and learning. (The latter happens to *everyone* at some point, if not at multiple points, in their careers!) If you happen upon any of these feelings, our recommendation is the same for unraveling: Take a break! You deserve it. Take time away, go do something that brings you joy, and come back fresh. Remember: This process doesn't define you.

The same is true for anyone who receives a score report that wasn't what they were hoping for. A low score doesn't mean you're a bad teacher, and it's a mistake to make that correlation. When scores come in, there is no rule that you must immediately make a decision concerning your next step. In this situation, take a deep breath and look at the first part of Chapter 10. That section can give perspective and ideas for what to do next.

Common Overall Pitfalls ◆ 47

❓ Case Study Practice

Considering the points in this chapter, what significant errors did each of these teachers make in their submission?

> **Example 1:** For the C4 prompt, "What and who were the sources for the information that you gathered? What guided you in selecting those particular sources of information?" ("Component 4 Instructions and Scoring Rubric," National Board for Professional Teaching Standards 12). Ms. Day included answers from student and parent surveys, as well as proficiency level data from a district exam that her new level 2 students took at the end of level 1 last year. She was feeling great that she was able to use both quantitative and qualitative data, both of which were related to her unit goals, to answer the question. Feeling like she knocked it out of the park, she moved on.

Ms. Day's Error:

> **Example 2:** Mr. Belding is so busy! He's a parent, a husband, a coach, a full-time teacher, and he serves on three committees at school. He is a veteran teacher, so some days, when he doesn't have enough time to plan, he just wings it. Because he has successfully taught for 20 years (and students love him!), it always turns out well, and he can tell students have made progress. The morning of the C3 lesson video recording, he realized he didn't like what he used last year for this lesson and found something he liked better online. He downloaded it (it even came with a teacher guide!), he taught it as prescribed, and the students were engaged during the entire recording. Whew!

Mr. Belding's Error:

Example 3: Mrs. Calypso was reflecting on her students' summative assessment results versus the formative assessment results. She was so pleased with how they did, and she was excited to write about it! She wrote about her level 1 students "struggling" with the formative assessment and wrote, "Many lack basic skills." On the unit summative assessment, however, she glowed with pride, stating that her students "showed remarkable improvement" and "made great progress."

Mrs. Calypso's Error:

Example 4: Mr. Kimble read the C2 prompt "What were the goals of the instructional sequence that preceded this assessment?" and had questions about it. What do they mean by goals? Should this be vocabulary-focused? Grammar-focused? Proficiency level-focused? Something social-emotional in nature? Should it be a goal for the whole class or for only the selected students? And how should he write the goals? Since he was confused, he decided to write goals that answered each of the questions he was wondering about. He felt sure this would cover all the bases.

Mr. Kimble's Error:

 ## Case Study Analysis

Let's examine each teacher's error.

Example 1: Ms. Day is right to be happy that she obtained relevant and related data to support her goals. The problem is she only replied to the first clause of the prompt (description); she did not elaborate by stating what guided her selection of this data (analysis). This pitfall may prevent her from scoring well on the rubric.

Example 2: Mr. Belding's story is not dissimilar to many of those reading (or writing!) this book. When you've been a successful teacher for several years, and you know your content and students well, it's easy to "wing it" and still be successful! Sometimes we *need to* because we simply can't do everything for everyone all the time. But Mr. Belding's pitfall was a lack of planning and proper preparation. While it's not a problem to buy or borrow materials someone else made, it is a problem that he didn't have time to modify it for his unique classroom context this year.

Example 3: It's wonderful Mrs. Calypso's students did so well and made progress! What's *not* wonderful is Mrs. Calypso's pitfall: lack of specificity. *How* did the students struggle, with *what*, and how did she *know*? What were the basic skills they lacked? How did they improve? In what ways? She should have included specific quantitative data (e.g., test scores) and/or qualitative data (e.g., student comments to justify her decision-making for these students.)

Example 4: Mr. Kimble fell into the pitfall of overthinking straightforward questions, and this caused him to lack focus. As a result, he (likely) took up far too much of his allotted space listing too many goals. He was casting too wide a net, so it is probable that these goals weren't all connected to each other or to his instructional plan. Don't overthink what "the NBPTS wants"; what they *want* is for you to tell them what *you* did and *why*.

We all make mistakes, and your path to becoming an NBCT will inevitably include some mistakes. That's normal and, with any luck, you'll learn from them. We hope this chapter, combined with the pitfalls specific to individual components in Section 2, will help mitigate some of the most common errors.

References

National Board for Professional Teaching Standards. *Early Adolescence through Young Adulthood/World Languages: Component 4 — Effective and Reflective Practitioner.* Prepared by Pearson under contract with the National Board for Professional Teaching Standards, © 2021, *National Board for Professional Teaching Standards*, https://www.nbpts.org/certification/candidate-center/first-time-and-returning-candidate-resources/#candidate-instructions. Accessed 7 Aug. 2025.

SECTION 2
The Four Components

6

Component 1

Content Knowledge

Part 1: Selected Response Questions

We asked NBC candidates, "What was the most frustrating or challenging part of the certification process?" Maybe you can identify with this:

> Studying for the C1 test for months, then getting to the testing facility and seeing the questions. Realizing I had studied 1/3 of the questions and content.
> —Krista L., NBCT since 2021

We hear this a lot! Given the high stakes of the C1 selected response test, most candidates wish NBPTS provided more guidance on what and how to study. That's the bad news. The *good* news—which many candidates overlook—is that NBPTS *has* given us World Language Standards, which are covered on the test. Take time to read these standards carefully; there's a lot there. C1 measures NBPTS Standard II (Knowledge of Language) and Standard IV (Knowledge of Language Acquisition) ("Component 1 Instructions and Scoring Rubric,", National Board for Professional Teaching Standards 1). We've fleshed out those two standards with concepts we believe are key. Most likely, you already know many of these items! Check those off! If there are terms that are new to you (or, like us, it's been decades since

DOI: 10.4324/9781003716860-8

you thought about them), spend time brushing up. Finally, while we believe this guide is helpful, it is not endorsed by NBPTS and may or may not reflect the actual test content.

General Tips

In C1, you have 60 minutes to answer 45 multiple choice questions. That's a little over one minute per question—not a lot of time! These general testing strategies may be helpful as you prepare:

- Each question has four possible answers. Read them all and eliminate any you know are wrong. Then make your best choice.
- Answer every question. There is no penalty for wrong answers.
- Since all questions have the same point value, work through the test quickly to pick up as many "easy" points as you can. You don't want to run out of time and miss an easy one!
- If you're unsure about a question, flag it. Then mark your best answer and move on. After you have worked through the test once, review the flagged questions. Don't spend more than one minute dithering over any answer on your first pass through the test.
- When in doubt, choose the answer with a more student-centered, proficiency, or cultural focus.
- If English is not your first language, we *strongly* encourage you to request the extra time accommodation.

So what should you actually study? Based on the NBPTS Standards (which you've already read, right?), these concepts stand out.

Knowledge of Language (Standard II)

1: Phonological Systems

This refers to the sounds in a language. For example, the English phonological system includes the sound /th/, which is not found in French or Spanish.

The French phonological system includes nasal vowels, the French/r/sound, h muet vs. h aspiré, and liaison obligatoire. Review the rules!

The Spanish phonological system includes soft consonants (the/d/and/t/are softer than English), the hard/h/sound in the back of the throat (in words with the letter "j"), and the rolled/r/ sound. "B" and "V" are pronounced almost identically in most Spanish dialects. Spanish phonology has numerous dialects, such as the Argentinian pronunciation of the "y" and "ll" sound (more of a/zh/sound) and the pronunciation of the letter "s" in Spain (more of a/th/sound).

Think about your target language (TL). How does the sound system differ from English? It may help to review the alphabet, or to consider which sounds your English-speaking students have trouble with in the TL, and which sounds TL speakers wrestle with when learning English. Those questions will help you identify major differences.

Your Turn!

What are some features we didn't mention about the Phonological System in your TL?

-
-
-
-

There may be questions in C1 asking you to identify differences in pronunciation, student spelling mistakes based on phonological systems, or questions comparing your TL to English. For questions like these, pronouncing the words to yourself and thinking about the relationships of the sounds may help you figure out the best answer.

2: Knowledge of How Language Works

This includes many subfields of linguistics, such as semantics, phonology, and morphology. (If only there was a "teen-ology," we would all have a Ph.D!) For many of us, these terms sound vaguely familiar, but we haven't used them since college.

✎ Your Turn!

Brush up on these *real* linguistic terms, and then jot an example or two from your TL.

Phonetics: how speech sounds are physically produced ... which we teach in class! Phonetics looks at factors such as the position of the tongue and lips and where the sound is generated (e.g., in the back of the throat, in the nasal cavity, in the front of the mouth).

Example: The English sounds /d/ and /t/ are produced almost identically, with the tongue touching the alveolar ridge behind the teeth. The only difference is the voicing: /d/ is voiced while /t/ is voiceless (or pronounced without vibrating the vocal cords).

My TL Examples:

Phonology: the patterns of how sounds go together in a language.

Example: In English phonology, words never begin with the sound /pt/, even though this sound exists at the end of words like "apt." So when English speakers see words like pterodactyl or the name Ptolemy, they usually drop the "p."

My TL Examples:

Morphology: how words are structured in a language. A "morpheme" is the smallest part of a word that carries meaning. Prefixes and suffixes are examples of morphemes.

Example: In English, the suffix "ed" carries the meaning "in the past." The letter "s" carries the meaning of "more than one." The short word "reactor" includes three morphemes ("re," "act," and "or"), but the longer word "porcupine" only has one morpheme!

My TL Examples:

Syntax: how sentences are structured in a language, typically related to word order.

Example: In English syntax, adjectives come before the words they describe, and object pronouns are usually at the end of the sentence. In Romance languages, adjectives are usually placed after the noun, and object pronouns can be placed before the verb. Students may transfer the syntax of their first language onto the TL, producing weird sentences like "To me, it is nice the dog brown" instead of "I like the brown dog."

My TL Examples:

Semantics: the meaning(s) a word carries. This is often related to words with multiple definitions.

Example: When your students tell you, "Bruh, that's sick!" you must determine the semantics of the word "sick." Does the student believe you are ill, or do they think your lesson is wonderful?

My TL Examples:

Semantic range: the variety of ways a single word can be used.

Example: The English word "track" can mean "a physical pathway" (e.g., a running track), the action of following something (e.g., to track a package through the mail), or a footprint (e.g., an animal track). When students choose the wrong translation from a dictionary, it is often because they didn't account for the semantic range of the word they looked up.

My TL Examples:

Pragmatics: how context impacts language interpretation (e.g., tone, inferences, reading between the lines). Using figures of speech to soften unpleasant topics is one use of pragmatics.

Example: In the American South, people often say "Bless your heart." The actual words mean nothing—there is no religious ritual of blessing someone's cardiac organ. This phrase may be used as a friendly filler when the speaker isn't sure what to say. However, when using a sarcastic tone, the phrase can indirectly suggest the listener is an idiot.

My TL Examples:

Etymology: the origin of words and how their usage has changed throughout history.

Example: The English word "naughty" came from the word "naught" or nothing. English speakers felt misbehaving children were acting out because of poverty; therefore, they were acting "naughty." Over time, this word lost its economic connotation and came to mean "badly behaved."

My TL Examples:

Historical Linguistics: broad changes in language over time. As you study, be aware of examples of major historical shifts in your TL.

Example: Medieval English used "thou" for a singular and "ye" for plural subject pronouns. Over time, these two merged into the pronoun "you," used for both singular and plural.

My TL Examples:

Socio-linguistics: how different subsets of society use language. Slang, generational distinctions, and different dialects fall into this field.

Author's Personal Example: During her daughter's wedding rehearsal, Lisa mentioned giving away the bride and then sitting down as a spectator, "hits different" when it's your own daughter. This made her kids laugh, since "Hits Different" is a Taylor Swift song, and they didn't expect to hear their Gen X mom say it.

My TL Examples:

3: Cultural Values

This refers specifically to how culture impacts language use. For example, in some English-speaking cultures, it's considered rude for a child to address an adult by their first name, reflecting an expected level of respect between age groups. In Cameroon, parents are called by the name of their oldest child (e.g., Ma

Bernadette, Pa Baptiste), reflecting the strong cultural emphasis on having children (and the accompanying change in identity). French culture places a high value on "Académie Française-approved" language, leading to events like national dictées. In both France and in northwest South America, there is a strong expectation to greet people when you see them; thus, the French tend to greet shopkeepers upon entering a business, while Ecuadorians will say "Buen provecho" when they see someone eating, whether they know them or not. Colombians tend to value formality, so they are more likely to use "usted" and will respond "pa'su merced" ("for your mercy") as an affirmative answer to a request.

Your Turn!

Identify some values in your target culture that impact language use.

4: Rhetorical and Stylistic Devices

Think of your middle school Language Arts class. Remember all the techniques you learned in the poetry unit to elicit reader reactions: simile, metaphor, imagery, allegory, irony, and sarcasm? Those are rhetorical and stylistic devices, and NBPTS expects you to be able to identify them in action. Is your highlighter ready? This is our list of 20 key terms, including examples for each in italics.

Simile: Comparing two unrelated items using the words "like" or "as". *Knowing what to study for the C1 selected response test is as hard as lunch duty on the day before winter break.*

Metaphor: Comparing two unrelated items using the verb "to be" (saying x is y). *This chapter is a treasure trove of study tips*

Analogy: Comparing two unrelated items to clarify or illustrate. *Learning Spanish is like riding a bike. You start slow and sometimes you scrape your knees, but all the pain leads to amazing freedom!*

Hyperbole: Exaggeration to make a point. *Studying for C1 is worse than teaching 7th graders with no deodorant after PE class.* (Clearly, *nothing* is worse than that!)

Understatement: Describing something as less important or dramatic than it is to make a point. *When a mouse ran through the classroom, it was mildly disruptive to Mr. Miyagi's C3 video lesson.*

Anecdote: A short story to illustrate a point. *Dr. Jones told his students how he had failed to obtain some lost artifacts for a museum as a teenager. This event motivated him to take extreme measures to ensure archeological treasures stay available to the public.*

Allusion: Hinting at a well-known or common idea without saying it directly. *The previous example is an allusion to the movie* Indiana Jones and the Last Crusade.

Allegory: A work of art that is symbolic of a deeper truth. *Animal Farm is an allegory for the evils of Stalin's U.S.S.R.*

Satire: A written work intended to mock or insult. *Any and all articles from The Onion are satires on current politics and culture.*

Personification: Giving human or animal traits to inanimate objects. *I don't understand how pencils just get up and walk out of my classroom!*

Sarcasm: Saying the opposite of what you mean, often with a biting tone. *I should invest in a pencil factory. I would be a millionaire!*

Parallelism: Using similar structures to highlight a comparison. *The world will little note, nor long remember what we say here, but it can never forget what they did here… that government of the people, by the people, for the people, shall not perish from the earth (Gettysburg Address, Abraham Lincoln)*

Pun: Using a word with multiple meanings in a surprising/funny way. *There's a hole in my grocery bag? Must've been the sharp cheddar!* (Most "dad jokes" use puns…)

Euphemism: An indirect phrase used to soften a harsh statement. Languages often have euphemisms for sensitive topics like death, bodily functions, and money. *"She went to the powder room"* is an indirect way to say *"She's peeing."*

Imagery: Descriptive language used to help the reader visualize a scene. *I wandered lonely as a cloud/That floats on high o'er vales and hills... (William Wordsworth)*

Paradox: Two ideas that cannot be true at the same time, but illustrate a larger point. *You have to spend money to make money.*

Antithesis: The total opposite. *That's one small step for man, one giant leap for mankind. (Neil Armstrong)*

Rhetorical question: A question asked for emotional impact or to make a point, not because it is meant to be answered. *What's in a name? That which we call a rose/By any other name would smell as sweet. (Romeo and Juliet, William Shakespeare)*

Alliteration: Using the same sound repeatedly. *While I nodded, nearly napping, suddenly there came a tapping,/As of someone gently rapping, rapping at my chamber door. (The Raven, Edgar Allen Poe)*

Anaphora: Repeating a phrase at the beginning of several clauses to emphasize a point. *We shall fight on the beaches, we shall fight on the landing grounds, we shall fight in the fields and in the streets, we shall fight in the hills; we shall never surrender... Winston Churchill, 1940*

Your Turn!

Think of an example of each literary device (in English or in your TL)

- allusion
- euphemism
- parallelism
- analogy
- alliteration
- metaphor
- antithesis
- understatement
- pun
- rhetorical question
- imagery

- anecdote
- paradox
- satire
- simile
- anaphora
- personification
- allegory
- hyperbole
- sarcasm

5: Geographical Variations

Review some major dialects of your TL and be aware of commonly-known vocabulary or pronunciation differences.

French Examples

- The Swiss dialect (e.g., numbers *septante*, *huitante*, and *nonante*, German-inspired pronunciation of "w")
- The Quebecois dialect (e.g., unique vocabulary such as *breuvage*, *char*, *magisiner*, *souper*; rejection of some anglicisms such as using *un chien chaud* instead of *un hot dog*; contraction of *je suis* to *chu*; distinctive vowel sounds)
- Verlan slang (e.g., *meuf* (femme), *teuf* (fête), *tromé* (métro), *ouf* (fou))
- Arabic influence on French (e.g., *kiffe* as slang for *like*; many words for plants and animals such as *jasmin*, *pastèque*, and *gazelle*)
- English influence on French, especially for words related to technology and pop culture (e.g., *l'internet*, *un jean*, *la musique rock*)
- My idea: _____

Spanish Examples

- Influence of Arabic due to the Moorish conquest in the Middle Ages (e.g., many words for plants and animals, such as *naranja*, *zanahoria*, *atun*, and *jirafa*; many words beginning with *al* or containing the letter *z*, such as *azucar*, *taza*, *áljebra*, *algodón*).

- Spain dialect (e.g., use of *vosotros*, unique pronunciation of the *s* sound).
- Influence of indigenous languages in Mexico (e.g., many words for plants such as *aguacate, cacahuete, chicle*; many geographical locations; *mole, popote*).
- Influence of Italian on Argentine Spanish (e.g., lunfardo slang words such as *mina* (woman), *laburar* (work), and *pibe* (friend))
- Vesre slag (reversing syllables; e.g., *chele* (milk), *gomía* (amigo))
- Dialects of isolated communities of "hispanos" in the Southwestern United States that still speak a version of Spanish descended from the conquistadors
- Words which are fine in some dialects but lewd in others (e.g., coño, pendejo)
- Voseo: the use of "vos" instead of "tú" in countries such as Argentina and Uruguay, which also influences how verbs are conjugated (e.g., Tú hablas → Vos hablás, Tú tienes → Vos tenés, Tú vienes → Vos venís)
- English influence on Spanish, especially for pop culture and technology terms (e.g., los jeans, el internet, chequear)
- My idea: _____

6A: Current Trends in the Development of the TL

Think of some current changes or debates related to your TL. Examples:

- Current slang
- Formal changes by the Academy of your language (e.g., French Academy spelling changes of 1990, Royal Spanish Academy changes to the alphabet in 2010)
- Discussions around gendered language (e.g., use of *latinx* in Spanish, addition of professions for both genders in French, use of gender neutral pronouns)
- My idea: _____

6B: Comparison of English and the TL

This includes the concept of language transfer, the tendency of learners to apply the rules of their first language to the new language. Language transfer is behind many errors our students make. For example:

- Mistakenly using 's for possession (e.g., Paco's perro es muy amable/Pierre's chien est très agréable).
- Errors with adjective placement (e.g., una fácil clase/ un facile cours).
- Errors with object pronouns (e.g., Yo doy el a ella./ Je donne le à elle).
- In Spanish, difficulty with the verb "gustar" (e.g., Yo gusta el pollo).
- In French, negation errors. (e.g., Je no aime le fromage).
- My idea: _____

How might you correct these and similar errors? In general, as a learner has more encounters with the correct structure, errors gradually extinguish. The teacher can also use "recasting" (i.e., restating the student's phrase correctly). For example, if the student says "Es Paco's gato," the teacher might reply, "Oh qué bueno. Es el gato de Paco."

Knowledge of Language Acquisition (Standard IV)

NBPTS uses ACTFL's frameworks throughout C1, so it is worth taking time to familiarize yourself with ACTFL's expectations (read more in Chapter 2 and at actfl.org). Additionally, NBPTS identifies these areas that may be tested in C1.

1: Current Theories and Research

The most influential theory in U.S. education is Dr. Stephen Krashen's theory of Second Language Acquisition (SLA). This overview is meant to give you a taste of Krashen's approach to language instruction and its classroom implementation.

Krashen has five major hypotheses:

- Acquisition-Learning Hypothesis: Language should be acquired organically as learners are exposed to it, as opposed to memorizing vocabulary and rules. This is sometimes called Language Acquisition (which happens unconsciously) vs. Language Learning (which is conscious).
- Monitor Hypothesis: Language learners use their understanding of grammar—their internal *monitor*—to make their own language production as correct as possible. When a student self-corrects, this is a sign that they are optimally monitoring their language production.
- Input Hypothesis: The language instructor should provide input that is just one step more advanced than the learner's current proficiency.
- Natural Order: Learners acquire grammatical concepts in a predictable order as they are exposed to language input over time. For some learners, this natural order includes a "silent period" where they are taking in language but not yet producing it.
- Affective Filter: This refers to the learner's emotional state. If the learner's affective filter is high (e.g., the learner feels worried, anxious, angry, etc.), their ability to produce language decreases. A low affective filter means the learner feels comfortable and unthreatened, and their ability to produce language increases.

Case Study Practice

Which aspect of Krashen's SLA theory applies to these classroom situations? Why?

> **Example 1:** Paula has been in class for several weeks and clearly understands some classroom commands like "Take out your laptop" and "Let's line up." Miss Honey

has tried to include Paula in class by asking simple questions, but Paula just shakes her head and refuses to answer.
Aspect & Rationale:

Example 2: Miss Vaughn taught her students how to use "apostrophe s" to show possession, and her kids did well on the test. She is confused as to why students are still making mistakes with this construction and saying things like, "This is the dog of my brother."
Aspect & Rationale:

Example 3: Isabelle memorized her poem in French. But when she tried to recite it in front of the class, she stumbled over her words and had terrible pronunciation.
Aspect & Rationale:

Example 4: Marcos was arranging to meet his friend for coffee. He said, "I will meeting you…. I will meet you at 3:00."
Aspect & Rationale:

Example 5: Dr. Jones believes in Krashen's theory of language acquisition, so on the first day of class he speaks quickly and 100% in the TL.
Aspect & Rationale:

Case Study Analysis

Let's take a look at how Krashen's approach relates to these classroom scenarios.

> **Example 1:** Paula is likely experiencing a "silent period" where she is absorbing, but not yet producing, the TL. With patience and time, Paula will naturally begin speaking as she acquires more language.
>
> **Example 2:** Miss Vaughan is teaching using a "language learning" theory rather than Krashen's idea of "language acquisition." Her students' mistakes suggest they need more input (i.e., more examples) of the possessive construction.
>
> **Example 3:** Isabelle is feeling nervous, so her affective filter is high. This causes her language production to drop. Most likely, she will be able to recite the poem perfectly— later, to herself, at home in the shower.
>
> **Example 4:** This self-correction is exactly what we want to see from learners. Marcos is working toward accuracy, but this is not preventing him from communicating his ideas in the TL.
>
> **Example 5:** Dr. Jones should review Krashen's Input Hypothesis. Language input must be just a bit beyond learners' current proficiency level for acquisition.

Familiarity with Krashen's SLA theory can be applied throughout your NBC portfolio entries and represents current best practices in language instruction.

2: Learner Characteristics

ACTFL's "proficiency pyramid" describes characteristics of learners as they progress in language study.

- ♦ Novice Learners: operate at the word level
- ♦ Intermediate Learners: operate at the sentence level
- ♦ Advanced Learners: operate at the paragraph level

There are two more levels: superior and distinguished. However, most K-12 students will be working at Novice and Intermediate levels, so we recommend you focus on these. Each level is further broken down into low/mid/high, based on how consistently and comfortably the learner maintains the qualities of that level. So students may be working at a "novice mid" (NM) or "intermediate low" (IL) level. NBPTS assumes candidates are familiar with these levels and know the characteristics of learners at each. (Don't believe us? Check out how many times this terminology appears in the sample questions!) You can learn more about these proficiency levels at www.actfl.org.

Case Study Practice

As you read each student's profile, identify their proficiency level. How can you tell?

> **Example 1**: Gabby is describing her weekend. "This weekend I went Grandma's house. I went with family. Mom, dad, uncle, cousin. Two cousin. Eat food. Much, much good food. Family is much fun."

Proficiency Level & Rationale:

Example 2:
Marcus: I have cousin. New baby. Tuesday. Is cute. Is very… wahh!
Teacher: Is your baby cousin loud?
Marcus: Yes. Loud.
Teacher: Is your cousin a boy or a girl?
Marcus: Is girl. Little, little.

Proficiency Level & Rationale:

Example 3: Daniel is ordering in a restaurant.
Daniel: I would like a roast beef sandwich and apple juice.
Server: And for your side?
Daniel: What do you have?
Server: We have potato chips or steamed broccoli.
Daniel: Please give me potato chips.
Server: Do you want that on white or wheat?
Daniel: Umm… excuse me?
Server: What kind of bread do you want? White or wheat?
Daniel: Umm… I'll take wheat.

Proficiency Level & Rationale:

Example 4:
Teacher: Do you like vegetables?
Edwin: Yes. Like vegetables.
Teacher: What is your favorite vegetable?
Edwin: Uhh…
Teacher: Do you like carrots? Do you like beans?
Edwin: Yes. Yes. Carrots. Beans. Like.

Proficiency Level & Rationale:

Case Study Analysis

Example 1: Gabby is beginning to construct her own sentences. She has a lot of errors and struggles to express her ideas, hallmarks of intermediate low learners.

Example 2: Marcus has characteristics of a Novice high speaker. He uses mainly memorized words and phrases, but is able to begin expressing his own ideas. When Marcus needs the unknown word "loud," he is stuck and needs outside input to get his idea across.

Example 3: Daniel is moving toward Intermediate High proficiency. He handles predictable exchanges with confidence, but when he encounters unfamiliar language, he is a bit stuck. Daniel has good coping skills and can ask for clarification. It's unclear whether he really understood his choice of wheat bread, but he's open to the adventure!

Example 4: Edwin is at the very beginning of his language study, probably at novice low. He responds with simple, memorized phrases, but he cannot produce original language.

3: Learning Styles

Visual, Auditory, and Kinesthetic (hands-on) is a common learning style model that suggests information can be presented in these three modes. There is some evidence that individuals learn better in one modality than the others, and if you teach middle school, you might believe hands-on is the *only* way your kids learn! A second important learning style theory, Howard Gardner's Multiple Intelligences, posits that there are different ways of being intelligent and students learn best when working in the intelligence that suits them. There were originally seven intelligences in Gardner's theory: linguistic, logical, visual-spatial, bodily-kinesthetic, musical, interpersonal, and intrapersonal. He has since expanded his model to include even more. There will be many opportunities to show how you meet students' learning styles as you complete your NBC portfolio.

4: Instructional Strategies

These are a few influential world language instructional strategies:

♦ Proficiency-based learning: A focus on what learners are able to do with the TL vs. what they know about the language. At the end of a proficiency-based unit, learners should be able to complete an assigned task (e.g., make a purchase, narrate a past event).

♦ TPR (Total Physical Response): An acquisition-based language method in which learners respond to commands with a physical action.

- TPRS (Teaching Proficiency through Reading and Storytelling): An acquisition-based method where the teacher and learners create a story together using the TL.
- Inductive Learning/Inquiry Learning: An acquisition-based strategy where learners examine a TL source to figure out vocabulary or structures.
- Grammar in Context: Language instruction that introduces grammar organically as it is needed to complete proficiency-based tasks, rather than introducing it in isolation through direct instruction and drills.
- Project-Based Learning (PBL)/Integrated Proficiency Assessments (IPAs... not beer!): A method where content is embedded in meaningful projects with real-world applications.

5: Competencies and Discourse Features

This includes ACTFL's modes of communication:

- Interpretive reading: Comprehending a written text in the TL
- Interpretive listening: Comprehending audio in the TL
- Interpersonal speaking: A two-way verbal exchange (e.g., a conversation, an exchange between customer and service provider)
- Interpersonal writing: A two-way written exchange (e.g., texting)
- Presentational speaking: Speaking to an audience (e.g., a speech, a personal introduction, an announcement)
- Presentational writing: Writing for an audience (e.g., an essay, a poster, an advertisement)

An effective language class incorporates each of these communicative competencies.

Discourse features are a fancy term for "Communicating meaning without literal words." Examples include tone, volume, pace of speech, register, use of fillers, transitions between topics, interruptions, and figurative language.

6: Cultural Knowledge

Consider reviewing ACTFL's framework for understanding cultures, including:

- Products: Physical (e.g., foods, clothing, furnishings) or intangible (e.g., songs, dances) items that are part of a culture
- Practices: Common activities in a culture (e.g., rites of passage, daily routines)
- Perspectives: Underlying beliefs or values that influence members of a culture (e.g., time orientation, individualism vs. collectivism, views of authority)

Next Steps

Are you feeling encouraged? Most likely, you already knew a lot of this—and maybe now you remember a few things you'd forgotten! If you need more practice, many of these topics are widely discussed online. Social media can be a perfect source to learn about different dialects and cultural trends in your TL, while blogs and teacher forums can illuminate how these ideas are implemented in class. Finally, try prompting AI to give you some practice multiple choice questions! You can make your prompts as specific as you like to home in on the content you'd like to practice.

Part 2: Constructed Response Questions

When C1 transitions from the Selected Response section to the Constructed Response section, allow your brain to cue Jon Bon Jovi—"Whooooaaaaaa! We're halfway theeeeeere!"—because this shift marks the halfway point in C1! Not only are you halfway through the test, but what you just did and what you're about to do each account for exactly 50% of the C1 total score (1).

While the NBPTS prefers to call this the "Construction Response (CR)" section, that's just a fancy way of saying "essay test." Candidates write three 30-minute essays in English, and we strongly recommend to take the extended time offered if English is not your first language. (30 minutes go by fast, so don't be shy! It's better to ask for it and not need it than to find out midway through that you should've asked for it.) Refer to the NBPTS guides or contact the NBPTS directly for more information.

Let's look at each CR question individually to gain understanding and create a plan of attack!

Constructed Response Question #1 (CR1)

Summary of CR1

CR1 begins with a sample of student work, and the goal is to evaluate your knowledge of language acquisition. The sample you see could reflect a student at the Novice, Intermediate, or Advanced level of language proficiency per ACTFL guidelines, so it's best to prepare yourself for any of them. After reading the student sample, you will choose one "significant" error to discuss, followed by a deeper dive into what you would do as that student's teacher to move them forward in their learning (2).

What You Will Turn In for CR1

This essay has three main parts: Step 1 is simply discussing a significant error you see. There may be more than one type of error, however, so pick *one* and make sure it's *significant*. Step 2 is explaining how this error relates to what's typical for a student at this level. The directions will tell you the level; you do not have to infer this. Step 3 is planning what you would do next for that student *based on* the error they are making at their proficiency level.

Planning for CR1

We believe the best studying for CR1 is simply being in the classroom and doing your day-to-day job because this question is literally what we do *every single day*! However, if it makes you too nervous to fall back on "This is what I DO!" —fair enough!— studying in a more concrete way is absolutely possible.

CR1 starts with an error, so we recommend making a long list of errors you see for each level of language learner: Novice, Intermediate, and Advanced. There will certainly be overlap among these errors, and that's okay. Next, go through and cross out any that don't feel "significant" for that level. For example, we argue that missing accents is a low-grade error at any level and is not substantive enough to write about. Significant errors often interfere with communication and/or the student repeatedly makes this error throughout the sample.

Showcase Your Theory: CR1

Step 2 of this question—explaining why this error is (or isn't) typical of this level of learner—is your opportunity to show assessors that you understand language acquisition and the typical progression of student learning.

You may want to consider including information such as:

- Which skills generally lead up to the error that was made
- Which skills often follow the error that was made
- Your experiences with your own students and this error
- Reasons why this error may occur
- My idea: _____

Your Turn!

Test your knowledge of language proficiency here. We recommend writing everything you know first; then, if needed, dig into ACTFL's website to round out any missing knowledge that feels important. This is a good way to test your current understanding versus what you need to study. Think: What can students do with language at this level?

Novice:

Intermediate:

Advanced:

Showcase Your Practice: CR1

Step 3 of this question—explaining how you would plan language instruction for this student—is your opportunity to show assessors that you understand best practice in world language teaching.

Your answer could include information such as:

- ♦ Vocabulary or structures that may need to be strengthened
- ♦ General types of activities that could support the student's growth
- ♦ Specific activities that could support the student's growth
- ♦ A timeline of steps (i.e., First, I would X; Then I would Y; if the student is responding well and making progress, I would follow with Z)
- ♦ My idea: _____

With each of those items, the *why* is essential. If you include the reason *why* you would take a particular step with the student, it meshes your knowledge of language acquisition with a practical application (i.e., what you do with students in your classroom). This analysis will make your essay stronger.

✎ Your Turn!

Refer back to your list of errors, and pick out a couple from each proficiency level to analyze further. What are common, significant errors for this level? (If you have never taught this level, ask a colleague.) What makes them typical/significant? Based on this error, what would move the student along the path to proficiency?

Novice learner error
   Next step:

Intermediate learner error
   Next step:

Advanced learner error
   Next step:

Common Pitfalls for CR1

While you study for CR, keep in mind these common pitfalls:

- Choosing more than one error. The instructions specifically call for analyzing *one* error. Choose one you see repeatedly or one that interferes with communication.
- Drifting back and forth among the prompts. Because the prompt has three distinct parts, we recommend answering in three distinct paragraphs. This supports *clarity*, which the assessors are looking for, per the rubrics.
- Failing to create a strong connection between the error and your plan for this student. Your plan should illustrate this pattern: "The student made X error because of Y, so *as a result*, I am going to do Z because _____."
- Running out of time. Think, plan, write.

Practice for CR1

Fortunately, the best practice for CR1 is at your fingertips each day at school! We recommend using actual student samples of written work—from different proficiency levels—and using them to write practice essays. You can ask colleagues for writing samples from their students (with names blacked out) if you need work from a proficiency level that isn't currently present in your classroom. Time yourself while you write so you get used to the 30-minute time limit.

After you have written your essays (hopefully at least one for each proficiency level), the final step is to evaluate your own work with a discerning eye. We recommend printing out your essays and the rubrics and working through them point by point. If you have a mentor, colleague, or friend who is willing to "grade" them for you, that's even better! In that case, just be sure you:

- pick someone who is familiar with the NBC process.
- pick someone with a well-defined critical lens who will give it to you straight!
- are ready to hear *honest feedback* and act on it.

TABLE 6.1 Sentence starters and CR1 rubric checklist

Possible sentence starters from the prompts | CR1	Checklist directly drawn from the most applicable NBPTS CR rubric points (Please refer to the rubrics for precise wording, and also note the rubrics are holistic.)
An error this student made was… An example of this is… This is an error because… The student should have…because…	___ I described one error. ___ My description is accurate.
This error is (not) typical of this language proficiency level. I know this because… I see this type of error occur when…	___ I gave an in-depth explanation of how this error corresponds to the typical development pattern for language learners at this level.

(Continued)

TABLE 6.1 (*Cont.*)

The error showed me that the student needs…because…	___ I insightfully analyzed how the work sample will shape my planning.
I will accomplish this by…	
An appropriate next step is… because…	

"Component 1 Instructions and Scoring Rubric," National Board for Professional Teaching Standards 13. (This table is downloadable from the Routledge webpage for this book, which can be found here: resourcecentre.routledge.com/books/9781041205357.)

You've finished CR1, so here comes Bon Jovi again: *[you've] gotta hold on to what you've got (your CR1 answer)*! CR2 is coming: *We'll give it a shot! You live for the fight (NBC) when that's all that you've got!* WHOOOOAAAAA!

Constructed Response Question #2 (CR2)

Summary of CR 2

The second CR question focuses on your knowledge of a target language culture. This prompt is truly a deep dive into the products, practices, and perspectives present in the target language world (2).

What You Will Turn In for CR2

Like CR1, CR2 also has three main parts: Step 1 is describing a cultural topic in its proper context. Step 2 is insightfully explaining how the topic has influenced your target language world. The focus should be on *one* way the topic was influential. Step 3 is an in-depth analysis of the significance and legacy of your cultural topic. The basic steps are: describe, explain, and analyze.

Planning for CR2

CR2 centers around a cultural topic; therefore, we recommend you go back to list-making! Jot down a few cultural topics you know a little something about. The key is making sure the topics have enough depth and breadth, so consider topics that connect to multiple areas of society. For example, one significant person may have influenced the economy, politics, art, science, and history. Thinking through different aspects of your chosen topic gives you flexibility to use this knowledge to answer your exact CR2 question. We recommend you research and prepare two to three culturally significant topics, which gives you options on test day. When you have strong choices, you can avoid seeing the CR2 question, freezing, and thinking, "Holy Hannah … what I prepared does *not* work for this. What do I do *now?*"

One more word of advice: You want to demonstrate *expertise* in your cultural knowledge, so choose topics that show you know more about the target culture than the average upper-level student! For example, an essay on quinceañeras (a topic covered multiple times throughout Spanish study) may not impress assessors. On the other hand, choosing a little-known political figure or an art movement in a less well-known target culture demonstrates your unique expertise. Bonus points if you can teach assessors something new about the target culture! It's perfectly fine—and recommended, even!—to do some research as you prepare for CR2.

 **Your Turn!**

Choose three topics and write what you know about them in the context of the questions.

Topic #1

Which products of the culture does this topic relate to?

Which practices of the culture does this topic connect to?

Which perspectives of the culture does this topic connect to?

What are some social, historical, political, economic, intellectual, artistic, scientific, and/or geographic perspectives that connect to this topic?

Topic #2

Which products of the culture does this topic relate to?

Which practices of the culture does this topic connect to?

Which perspectives of the culture does this topic connect to?

What are some social, historical, political, economic, intellectual, artistic, scientific, and/or geographic perspectives that connect to this topic?

Topic #3

Which products of the culture does this topic relate to?

Which practices of the culture does this topic connect to?

Which perspectives of the culture does this topic connect to?

What are some social, historical, political, economic, intellectual, artistic, scientific, and/or geographic perspectives that connect to this topic?

These answers are the outline to your essay. Try pretending the assessors are attendees at a conference session you're giving on a cultural topic you're passionate about. You want to show what you know about this topic and why it's so valuable to know about—*clearly*, it's because it touches so many areas that we teach! This topic enriches everything else! This topic is *integral* to the target culture!

Common Pitfalls for CR2

During your preparation for CR2, consider these likely pitfalls:

- Failing to fact check during your planning. Your description of the cultural topic must be *accurate*.
- Providing only surface-level knowledge of the topic. Go deep!
- Failing to make connections across society.
- Choosing a topic you're not passionate about. This comes through in your writing!
- Running out of time. Think, plan, write.

Practice for CR2

For CR1, easy practice comes from evaluating student work. For CR2, it's all you! It's time to write three practice essays, focusing on the three main parts of the prompt, and using your notes from the Your Turn! Section. Set your timer to 30 minutes, and let's go!

TABLE 6.2 Sentence starters and CR2 rubric checklist

Planning prompts | CR2 These prompts are suggestions. This essay is broad in scope, so approaches will vary widely.	Checklist directly drawn from the most applicable NBPTS CR rubric points (Please refer to the rubrics for precise wording, and also note the rubrics are holistic.)
Strong intro sentence about my topic:	___ I identified a cultural topic related to the prompt. ___ My description is accurate.
This topic connects to ___ in the target culture by…	___ I gave an insightful explanation of how this topic relates to my target language world. ___ My response includes a product, a practice, and a perspective of the target language culture.
The influence of (this topic) expands into…by… (Repeat for several areas of influence.)	___ I wrote an in-depth analysis of the topic's significance and legacy in the target language world.

"Component 1 Instructions and Scoring Rubric," National Board for Professional Teaching Standards 16. (This table is downloadable from the Routledge webpage for this book, which can be found here: resourcecentre.routledge.com/books/9781041205357.)

Cue Bon Jovi again: *Take my hand (er, this book…), we'll make it I swear …* You only have one more essay to go!

Constructed Response Question #3

Summary of CR3

The final CR question merges curriculum, instruction, and culture, starting with a resource provided by the NBPTS. The objective is to create an original, student-centered, collaborative activity with another teacher from another discipline. This collaboration will include communication among students, a comparison of languages (target language and shared language of the students), and inclusion of discipline-specific content (2).

What You Will Turn In for CR3

Structurally, CR1 and CR2 are fairly cut and dried: They each have three main parts. CR3 is slightly different. CR3 has two main parts, but the second part is broken down into three requirements:

> Part 1: Describe anything you need to consider for instruction, based on the provided resource.
> Part 2: Design and describe a cross-curricular unit.
> Requirement 1: Students must communicate.
> Requirement 2: Students must make connections between the target language and their primary language.
> Requirement 3: You must integrate content from other disciplines.

Planning for CR3

CR3 is all about creativity in instruction, and you can let your imagination run wild! There is no single, correct way to write any of your constructed response essays, but if you feel like a bit of guidance is helpful, you've come to the right place!

First, you will read the prompt, preview the instructional resource provided, and write part one: a description of anything that should be considered for the instruction. This can easily be accomplished in narrative form or as a bulleted list. We don't believe either is better than the other, but if you choose a list format, it's crucial you *describe* the factors as opposed to only *listing* them. There are numerous factors to consider when planning instruction, and here are a few ideas:

- What do the students already know? (e.g., vocabulary, culture, grammatical structures)
- What do you have to teach before using the resource?
- What, if anything, in the resource could be problematic? (e.g., difficult vocabulary, unknown structures, unrelatable content)
- What resources are necessary and available?
- Who will you collaborate with? This must be a teacher from another discipline, but it does *not* have to be a discipline that actually exists at your school! You can make up your "ideal colleague" and "ideal class partnership"!
- Consider the partner class. What do *those* students already know, and what does their teacher need to teach before your students collaborate?
- What is the proficiency level of the students based on the prompt? Likely, the class you're collaborating with is going to be English-speaking, so the collaborative piece may be primarily in English, while the content in *your* class can be in the target language.
- How often will the classes collaborate? It doesn't have to be all day, every day.
- What is the structure of the class time? Again, you get to make this up! If you want 90-minute periods for this collaboration, you got 'em! 45-minute periods? Done!
- My idea: _____

Next, it's time to wow the assessors with your collaborative activity-planning prowess! There are diverse ways to approach Part 2; however, we recommend structuring your collaborative activity similar to how one would structure a sub plan. (A notable difference is that this wouldn't be quite as detailed as a sub plan, and your students in CR3 are angels!) We advocate for this approach because it is easy to provide clarity and structure to your response this way, but if a different approach suits you better, go for it—this is *your* CR3! If you choose to carry on with this method, you will organize by days of the week. For each day, write what you and your students will do, what your colleague and their students will do, and what everyone will do *together* (for the times that you're collaborating as a large group).

As you write your daily plan, include key information such as *why* you are doing what you're doing and what your goals are. This isn't explicitly stated in the directions provided by the NBPTS, but we believe it's part of being "insightful," which *is* in the directions. Also, remember you need a student-centered activity, meaningful communication, connections between the students' primary language and the target language of your class, and content from at least one other discipline. It may help to write those down on your scratch paper during the test so that you can check them off as you go, and it may help the *assessor* if you use that exact verbiage in your writing so it stands out to them.

Lastly, keep in mind there is no requirement for the two groups of students to be together all day, every day, of this collaborative unit; in fact, there's no requirement for how much they meet at all. You and your imaginary colleague can choose the best structure for your imaginary (and wonderfully inquisitive, good-smelling, and driven) students!

Common Pitfalls for CR3

- Experiencing paralysis of *reality*. Your actual teaching reality *does not matter* for CR3. You get to invent the students, colleague, unit, and materials that you want!
- Failing to address all parts of the prompt. Remember: It is not uncommon for the NBPTS to include more than one requirement per sentence, so it's wise to carefully analyze all clauses.
- Forgetting to incorporate the resource they provide.

- Forcing a daily collaboration if it doesn't feel right to you. Collaboration should enhance both classes, not just check a box.
- Rambling with a lack of structure. The prompt is quite open, so it's in your best interest to *plan* with ample organization.
- Running out of time. Think, plan, write.

Practice for CR3

For your CR3 practice essay(s), start with a resource. Ask a colleague to give you something from a class they teach but you don't (so the resource feels fresh!), find a resource online to practice with, or ask AI to build a resource for you. Any of those approaches would provide a new-to-you resource, mimicking your experience in the testing center. Once you have secured a resource, set the timer for 30 minutes again, and dig in!

TABLE 6.3 Sentence starters and CR3 rubric checklist

Possible sentence starters from the prompts | CR3	Checklist drawn directly from the most applicable NBPTS CR rubric points (Please refer to the rubrics for precise wording, and also note the rubrics are holistic.)
In order to effectively teach this unit, I need to consider … because…	___ I described factors to consider when designing instruction. ___ My descriptions were in-depth.
The basic activity is: This is student-centered because… I am integrating the provided resource by…	___ My activity is student-centered. ___ I insightfully explained how I would use the resource.
Students will connect the target language to the primary language of the class when they… Students will make these linguistic comparisons:	___ Students make connections and comparisons between their primary language and the target language.

(Continued)

Copyright material from Erin E. H. Austin and Lisa Bartels (2026), *Achieving National Board Certification in World Languages*, Routledge

TABLE 6.3 (*Cont.*)

Students will connect class content to (another discipline) when they…	___ Students make connections and comparisons with content from other disciplines.
Students will compare class content to (another discipline) when they…	
All students will communicate by (writing, speaking) about…	___ The students (of both classes) communicate and collaborate.
All students will collaborate (e.g., in small groups, in pairs) in order to…	

"Component 1 Instructions and Scoring Rubric," National Board for Professional Teaching Standards 21. (This table is downloadable from the Routledge webpage for this book, which can be found here: resourcecentre.routledge.com/books/9781041205357.)

When you finish the test, you will most likely be ready for a calorie fest, reality TV binge, or a nap—and definitely reward yourself with one or all three of these! However, before you dump the C1 experience from your brain, there's one more step you can take to help yourself: Leave a laptop or notebook in your car at the testing center. As soon as you're back in your vehicle, write down everything you can remember about C1, including questions you thought were easy and *especially* questions you struggled with. You can't share this information with anyone—ever. But if you *do* end up needing to retake C1, you will thank your past self for writing a personalized study guide for round 2. That's it! The Constructed Response section is *done*…as are our Bon Jovi references.

References

National Board for Professional Teaching Standards. *Early Adolescence through Young Adulthood/World Languages: Component 1—Content Knowledge.* Prepared by Pearson under contract with the National Board for Professional Teaching Standards, © 2016, *National Board for Professional Teaching Standards,* https://www.nbpts.org/certification/candidate-center/first-time-and-returning-candidate-resources/#candidate-instructions. Accessed 7 Aug. 2025.

7

Component 2

Differentiation in Instruction

Fraulein Maria knew her students well and was committed to their success. Mischievous Kurt was an active boy, so Maria created a class activity with Kurt in mind; students practiced vocabulary while jumping up and down stairs. Brigitta, on the other hand, was a quiet and studious child, so Maria's next class activity was a silent cultural reading. Both students found something in class to enjoy, and both achieved her goals for the unit! The entire class demonstrated their learning with a successful public festival performance as a summative assessment. Maria was certain that her variety of class activities would score well. *How do you solve a problem like Maria*'s (lack of understanding of differentiation)?

Summary of Component 2

In Component 2 (C2), candidates showcase their mastery of assessment practices and of differentiated instruction. Candidates choose meaningful instructional goals and develop formative and summative assessments (i.e., pre- and post-assessments) to measure student progress toward those goals ("Component 2 Instructions and Scoring Rubric," National Board for Professional Teaching Standards 7–9).

Additionally, candidates demonstrate their ability to differentiate instruction by selecting two students with different needs. Candidates show how they tailor instruction at every step to meet each student's unique needs, resulting in improved achievement (1). C2 rubrics do not stipulate a simple variety of class activities; they ask candidates to show how they tailor instruction for the two featured students. The "Showcase Your Practice: Differentiation" section in this chapter discusses this concept further.

What You Will Turn In

In C2, you will submit three documents:

- Contextual Information Sheet (one-page form)
- Written Commentary (up to 15 pages)
- Assessment Materials (up to seven pages of your content, plus two cover page forms) (C2 instructions, page 10)

Accomplished Portfolios

According to the C2 rubrics, we believe assessors are looking for evidence that you:

- Know your students very well
- Choose instructional goals based on these students' needs
- Develop and deliver valid assessments to measure student achievement
- Use assessment results to develop instruction
- Incorporate various instructional strategies
- Monitor student progress at every step
- Understand how language learning works and adapt instruction to move students forward, wherever they are in the process
- Tailor instruction for different student needs
- Provide effective feedback
- Implement a repeated process.

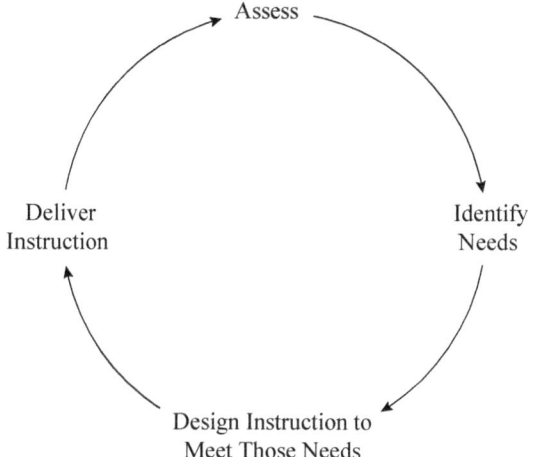

FIGURE 7.1 Continual Cycle Present in Accomplished Teaching

At every point, look for ways to show how you combine your knowledge of your individual students with your deep understanding of pedagogy to deliver *intentional* and *tailored* instruction.

Planning Your C2 Entry

As with all the Written Commentaries, C2 is rooted in your knowledge of your students. Using the guidance in Chapter 4 (time for a re-read, perhaps?), begin with a deep dive into your class. What are your students' unique characteristics, and what are their learning needs? Which handful of your delightful little weirdos stand out as good candidates for NBC experimentation? Don't gloss over this step; Knowledge of Students drives the rest of your C2 entry!

Next, home in on a few instructional goals that might work for your entry. Choosing appropriate goals is critical to your portfolio's success. Based on the C2 instructions, your goals should meet these criteria:

- You have several data points showing that *these* students need *these* goals at *this* moment in time.
- The goals are important to building language proficiency.

- You can teach the goals in three weeks to three months.
- You can articulate how the goals fit into the longer-term learning process.
- You know what came before this instructional sequence, why these goals are therefore important, and what the next instructional steps are likely to be.
- The goals are measurable. You can focus assessments to pinpoint students' achievement in relation to the goals. This, in turn, drives your instruction.
- You can implement a variety of instructional strategies to meet the goals.
- The goals lend themselves to incorporating the target culture.
- You are excited about teaching these goals! (This will come through in your writing… and in your work with students.)

(After choosing such out-of-this-world goals, now might be a good time to put out a tip jar in your classroom. Your students will certainly want to reward your unbelievable work, and who knows? Maybe you'll be able to buy a stamp as a result!)

While not an NBPTS requirement, we recommend bigger-picture or proficiency-focused goals rather than goals based on discrete structures or vocabulary sets. According to the C2 rubrics, selecting a goal of "minimal significance" earns a score of 2. Proficiency-based goals are, by definition, significant. They provide broader leeway to demonstrate your expertise, to showcase creative instruction, and to coach individual students. This will give you more to write about, in case you were worried about hitting 15 pages! Additionally, proficiency-based instruction is considered best practice in world language teaching. Thoughtfully describing why you used such an assessment is evidence of your accomplished practice.

✏️ Your Turn!

Brainstorm a few goals you might be able to use for C2.

>My students need…

>Based on this student data…

>Possible goal(s):

Showcase Your Theory: Assessment

Although the title of this component is "Differentiation in Instruction," the questions and scoring rubric are as much about assessment practices as differentiation. Don't believe us? The words "assess" or "assessment" appear 125 times in the C2 instructions, while variations of "differentiate" only appear 22 times! (Yes, we're the dorks who looked that up!) Thus, you must show expertise in both areas to score well on C2.

To provide evidence of accomplished assessment practices, you will bookend your instructional sequence with assessments to measure your chosen goals. If you use assessments that were written by someone else (such as a publisher), consider modifying them to meet your unique classroom situation. (Wayside doesn't know Sonia or Michael; show that *you* do!) Better yet, craft your own *original* assessments! Either way, articulate exactly why you selected the assessment for these students and for these goals.

"But we *have* to use common assessments within my department/district!" you might be thinking. Rationale limited to "This is the next test in the curriculum" or "This test is required by my school" may not score well on the C2 rubrics. If this is your situation, you can solve your conundrum in one of two ways. (1) Don't focus on the fact that the assessment is prescribed; simply write convincingly about why it's appropriate for these students. (2) Give an *additional* assessment, which you design and deliver specifically to meet the C2 requirements. Even for prescribed assessments, show how they are effective in measuring these students' unique situation and how your assessment usage reflects accomplished practice.

So what exactly qualifies as an "assessment"? While a traditional test is a tried-and-true technique, consider whether this is the best way to measure your students' progress. A less common type of assessment could demonstrate your expertise as an assessor and lead to more interesting results. (It could also lead to a nickel in that tip jar if the kids like it better!)

Possible assessment types:

- Traditional multiple choice, short answer, or essay questions
- A prepared or spontaneous speaking assignment
- A visual product (e.g., a comic strip, display, labeled image)
- A reading or listening activity
- Any type of project (e.g., individual, group, community-based, interdisciplinary)
- A portfolio
- A student self-assessment or reflection combined with any of the above
- A conference, verbal check-in, or exit ticket
- My idea: _____

See how fun this is? To add to everyone's enjoyment, don't forget a rubric for subjective assessments. You will write about your rationale for choosing these assessments in your Written Commentary, so break out the flair pens to track your thinking as you complete this step.

The goal of your formative assessment (or pre-assessment) is to collect data on what your students can and can't do before you start teaching. You will use these results to inform subsequent instruction. Choose your assessment thoughtfully. It should provide specific, measurable, and actionable data related to your unit goals, and should reveal a few areas where individual students can grow.

 **Your Turn!**

Using what you learned, brainstorm some possible formative assessments for your goals.

Possible formative assessment format

How this assessment relates to my instructional goals:

Why this assessment is appropriate for these students:

Your summative assessment (or post-instruction assessment) should also be valid, measurable, and specifically aligned to your goals (i.e., measuring student progress in the exact area you want to assess). You will analyze why it is appropriate for these students, how it connects to your goals, and how you used the data to measure student progress or achievement. The C2 instructions direct candidates to develop their summative assessment, including any rubrics or evaluation criteria, *before* planning instruction. This "backwards design" approach allows you to stay focused as you teach. Throughout the unit, you will monitor students' progress toward the skills on the summative assessment, adapting and tailoring instruction as you go.

❓ Case Study Practice

Using the "Showcase Your Theory" guidance, what errors did each teacher make in their summative assessment design?

>**Example 1:** Ms. Norbury wants to measure students' mastery of unit vocabulary, so she developed a quiz where students match English words with Spanish translations.
>
>**Ms. Norbury's Error:**

>**Example 2:** Ms. Watson asks her level 4 students to give a speech in Spanish about an environmental problem and its solution. When students finish, Ms. Watson verbally tells the student a few things they could do better and tells them what grade she is giving them.
>
>**Ms. Watson's Error:**

>**Example 3:** Miss Bliss is teaching students to interpret figurative language. She assesses students by asking them to name their favorite poem from the unit and to write several French sentences about how the poem impacted them.
>
>**Ms. Bliss' Error:**

>**Example 4:** Mr. Keating wants to evaluate students' knowledge of Spanish numbers. He provides several three-digit multiplication problems and asks them to write out the answers using Spanish words.
>
>**Mr. Keating's Error:**

Case Study Analysis

Let's examine each teacher's error:

> **Example 1:** C'mon, Norbster! Your students can do more than match words! Let them shine a bit with something more creative! (You can do it, woman!) A writing or speaking task using the vocabulary shows deeper learning, is more fun for students, and gives Ms. Norbury a lot more to write about in her C2 portfolio!
>
> **Example 2:** Ms. Watson better get ready for an avalanche of parent complaints! How will she justify why little Sophia got a C on her presentation? She needs to develop a rubric so everyone (students, parents, NBPTS assessors, and Ms. Watson herself) knows exactly what is being measured on this performance task.
>
> **Example 3:** Miss Bliss's assessment is not valid. Asking students to describe the emotional impact of their favorite poem has nothing to do with her goal of interpreting figurative language. She needs to go back to the drawing board and develop an assessment that will document her students' progress toward the goal.
>
> **Example 4:** Mr. Keating is asking students to complete extraneous tasks that were not taught in his unit. Any student who isn't a mathlete will automatically miss the questions, so Mr. Keating won't know whether the student doesn't know Spanish numbers or can't multiply. The result? Inactionable data. Mr. Keating needs to design an assessment that tests only students' mastery of numbers and nothing else.

Strong candidates choose appropriate, significant goals and ensure all assessments tightly align with those goals. They deliberately use assessment data to drive each instructional decision.

✎ Your Turn!

Using what you've learned, brainstorm some possible summative assessments for your unit.

    Possible summative assessment format:

    How this assessment relates to my instructional goals:

    Why this assessment is appropriate for these students:

    Ideally, when your students complete the summative assessment, you will see they've improved! Great job!

While your formative and summative assessments will be highlighted, C2 also prompts you to discuss how you monitor student growth during instruction (8). In other words, effective assessment is ongoing. In your Written Commentary, describe how you assessed students (formally and/or informally) throughout the unit. Then, analyze why you chose each assessment and how you used it to adjust instruction as you taught.

✎ Your Turn!

The following prompts may be helpful in documenting your ongoing assessments as you teach the unit.

    Assessment I used:

Why this assessment was appropriate:

What feedback I provided students:

How this assessment informed subsequent instruction:

For every assessment, you will show how you provided appropriate feedback to your students. Don't gloss over this step! Feedback is a critical component of assessment practice. As you plan, think about how you might provide intentional feedback to your selected students and why your choice is best for the situation. Could you give different feedback to different students, based on individual needs? Which errors will you correct, point out, or overlook? Will you foster student self-assessment and reflections, or will you correct all the work yourself? What might your conversations with students look like? How could you challenge, encourage, or motivate them? Will you hold students accountable to implement your feedback? These are practices you should plan for and write about in your entry. For each statement, don't forget to explain *why*.

Possible types of feedback:

- ♦ Grades (letter or numeric)
- ♦ Written comments
- ♦ Notes on a rubric

- Verbal or written corrections
- Conversations or a teacher conference
- Nonverbal signals (e.g., thumbs up, nodding while the student talks)
- My idea: _____

 **Your Turn!**

Brainstorm some feedback techniques you might implement for each of your assessments.

Formative Assessment

How I could provide feedback on this assessment:

Why this feedback is appropriate:

Summative Assessment

How I could provide feedback on this assessment:

Why this feedback is appropriate:

Informal Assessment(s)

How I could provide feedback on this assessment:

Why this feedback is appropriate:

Showcase Your Practice: Differentiation

Accomplished differentiation is the centerpiece of C2. Your two featured students are your case studies, providing a snapshot of your ability to effectively tailor instruction for individual needs. Differentiation is more purposeful than simply varying your activities for the full class. The idea is to guide two students down two unique instructional pathways, helping both to progress toward the same goals.

Your choice of featured students is key. You need to describe the two students in depth, drawing on data from multiple sources (as discussed in Chapter 4). Then, show how you diagnosed those students' unique needs in relation to your unit goals, and then designed an intentional and tailored series of lessons (what the NBPTS calls an *instructional sequence*) to meet those needs. At each step, remember to explain the *why*. Why do you know what the students need, and why are your selected activities appropriate?

In considering your selected students' needs, you might differentiate for:

- Language proficiency (e.g., native speakers, heritage speakers, prior language experiences, current target language proficiency, English proficiency)
- Student interest

- Personality (e.g., level of energy, introversion or extraversion)
- Learning preferences (e.g., preferred modality, multiple intelligences)
- Exceptionality (e.g., disability, giftedness)
- Social-emotional needs
- Career or long-term plans
- My idea: _____

It is wise to collect data on several students throughout your C2 unit of instruction. Murphy's Law suggests if you only collect data on two students (because that is the requirement), one of them will be out with mono, win the lottery and drop out of school, or get dumped and not be able to perform in class! When that happens, it's back to the drawing board for you!

Instead of tying your results to only two kids, we suggest differentiating for three to five students during your featured unit. Of course, this is more work, but it also gives you flexibility and insures your portfolio against teenage unpredictability. Pro tip: Find some pairs of students with similar needs and differentiate for them together. At the end of the unit, feature the two individuals who give you the best evidence to meet the C2 requirements.

Remember: As you finalize your student selection, you aren't tied to choosing the top two performers in your class (who might not have even needed you!). Expertly moving a struggling student forward is impressive teaching. Choose students who showed significant, unique, or substantial growth in your unit goals, thanks to your accomplished coaching and tailored instruction.

✎ Your turn!

Brainstorm some students you might feature in C2.

Student:

Differentiate for:

Possible differentiated activities:

Why these activities are appropriate:

Student

Differentiate for:

Possible differentiated activities:

Why these activities are appropriate:

Student

Differentiate for:

Possible differentiated activities:

Why these activities are appropriate:

Student

Differentiate for:

Possible differentiated activities:

Why these activities are appropriate:

Be creative and intentional as you develop personalized activities for your featured students. Some ways to differentiate a single concept may include:

- Giving choices
- Providing different source documents (e.g., different reading levels, different topics)
- Assigning different tasks to learn the same content
- Producing different products
- Having students develop content for others
- Connecting with communities of learners through in-person or virtual meetings
- My idea: _____

For each assignment, keep track of your thinking. Why did you select this activity for this specific student? How did you monitor your featured students' learning through repeated assessment, feedback, and adjustment to instruction? This data will form the backbone of your C2 Written Commentary.

Common Pitfalls

As you develop your C2 portfolio, take care to avoid these common pitfalls:

- Choosing too many goals. No one can keep track of all that! One to three proficiency-based goals is a good number.
- Providing an inappropriate rationale for your goals. Suggesting your goals were selected by someone else (like your department or district) will not convince assessors of your accomplished practice. Even if you are required to include particular content, use data from your students to show why, in your expert judgment, this material is an appropriate choice.
- Choosing goals that are too narrow. Your students can do more than memorize lists! Show your expertise in coaching them to communicate in the target language.
- Choosing goals that are too vague. Effective goals are specific and measurable. Goals such as "Get better in writing" or "Speak more comfortably" could be a starting point, but you will need to stipulate exactly what good writing or more comfortable speaking means for your students and how you will know when they've achieved it.
- Using a pre-made assessment as-is (e.g., a test from a textbook). If you use components from a pre-made assessment, show how you selected those components intentionally to align with your goals.
- Using assessments that are too vague. Your assessment should include a rubric or other objective measure.
- Using assessments that measure skills or content unrelated to your goals. Be focused.
- Providing inappropriate feedback or not writing about it in enough detail. Following each assessment, you should describe the feedback you provided to students, why you provided it, and how the feedback impacted student progress. *Many candidates overlook this point.*

- Correcting everything. Attacking student writing with a red pen is generally not effective. Instead, consider how you might incorporate a student-centered practice (e.g., focus on one type of error, incorporate student reflection and self-correction)
- Failing to incorporate culture. While only one question in the instructions asks about cultural integration, it is included in the C2 rubric. Incorporating some target-culture resources is likely to strengthen your entry.
- Failing to *actually* differentiate. Using a variety of activities in class to teach and learn multiple concepts can be fun and may be appropriate for other NBC components. However, this alone does not show you can differentiate *one* topic for *multiple* learners. Differentiation is creating multiple instructional pathways to the *same* goal.

Drafting Your Written Commentary

These sentence starters, adapted from the prompts in the NBPTS C2 Portfolio Instructions, will give you a starting point for drafting your Written Commentary. Be sure to *analyze* each step you take, using phrases like "because…," "this showed me…," and "I did this in order to…."

When you've completed the chart, read through it again (perhaps on a different day). Check each statement against the list on the right, adapted from the NBPTS C2 rubrics. Try to be clear-eyed in your self-assessment, as assessors cannot make inferences about your rationale; they can only score what you actually write.

TABLE 7.1 Sentence starters and C2 rubric checklist

Sentence starters from the prompts: Planning Instruction	Checklist drawn directly from the most applicable NBPTS C2 rubric points (Please refer to the rubrics for precise wording, and also note the rubric is holistic, so many points overlap with multiple prompts.)
Student A's formative assessment results led me to plan these learning experiences… because…	___ I used deep knowledge of my students to make informed decisions about instructional content.
Student B's formative assessment results led me to plan these learning experiences… because…	
My goals for this unit are…	___ I demonstrated a thorough knowledge of the language and of how language acquisition works. ___ I used this knowledge to set attainable and relevant learning goals for my students.

(Continued)

TABLE 7.1 (*Cont.*)

These goals are important and appropriate for student A because… (Include background info on this student. See Chapter 4.)	___ I used deep knowledge of my students to make informed decisions about instructional content.
	___ I drew upon knowledge of language acquisition to set attainable and relevant learning goals for my students.
These goals are important and appropriate for student B because… (Include background info on this student. See Chapter 4.)	___ I actively sought knowledge about all students' prior language experiences and used that knowledge in my instructional planning.
I plan to use these resources, technologies, and people in the unit. ♦ ♦ ♦ ♦ ♦ After each bullet, note why the resource is relevant to your lesson.	___ I adapted, created, and used appropriate resources to meet the needs of all my students. ___ I understand varied methodologies and approaches used in the teaching of languages. ___ I drew upon this knowledge to design instructional strategies appropriate for, and tightly connected to, the instructional goals and individual student needs.

(*Continued*)

TABLE 7.1 (*Cont.*)

Some other factors that influenced my planning were:	___ Any rubric point could be addressed here; strengthen any weak area.
How did your understanding of language acquisition influence your planning? Give specific examples. ♦ ♦ ♦	___ I demonstrate a thorough knowledge of the language and of how language acquisition works ___ I draw upon this knowledge to design instructional strategies appropriate for, and tightly connected to, the instructional goals and individual student needs.
Sentence starters from the prompts: Analysis of Instruction	**Checklist of the most applicable rubric points**
I used these instructional methods and strategies. ♦ ♦ ♦ ♦ ♦ After each bullet, note how the item relates to your goals and to your students' needs.	___ I understand varied methodologies and approaches used in the teaching of languages. ___ I draw upon this knowledge to design instructional strategies appropriate for, and tightly connected to, the instructional goals and individual student needs.

(*Continued*)

Copyright material from Erin E. H. Austin and Lisa Bartels (2026), *Achieving National Board Certification in World Languages*, Routledge

TABLE 7.1 (*Cont.*)

I varied my approach for Student A by… because… (Give specific examples.)	___ I used a variety of instructional approaches within an articulated sequence of instruction. ___ I set high expectations for all students in order to move students to more accomplished levels of performance.
I varied my approach for Student B by… because… (Give specific examples.)	
My instructional resources incorporated culture by….	___ I acquainted students with key cultural traits and concepts and helped them to synthesize and interpret this information in sensitive and meaningful ways.

(*Continued*)

TABLE 7.1 (*Cont.*)

During instruction I used these assessment strategies: ♦ ♦ ♦ ♦ ♦ After each bullet, note why you chose the assessment for these students at this time.	___ I understand varied methodologies and approaches used in the teaching of languages. ___ I drew upon this knowledge to design instructional strategies appropriate for, and tightly connected to, the instructional goals and individual student needs. ___ I drew upon my knowledge of students to design assessments.
I made these changes to my instruction based on the assessment results above: (specific examples with rationale) ♦ ♦ ♦ ♦ ♦ *Note: This question does not appear in the NBPTS C2 instructions, but it addresses the rubric point at right.*	___ I analyzed assessment results and made adjustments to curriculum and instruction based on my findings.

(*Continued*)

TABLE 7.1 (*Cont.*)

I provided appropriate feedback to student A throughout the unit by… (Give specific examples.)	___ I gave clear, insightful, and meaningful feedback to students.
I provided appropriate feedback to student B throughout the unit by… (Give specific examples.)	
Sentence starters from the prompts: Assessment 2	**Checklist of the most applicable rubric points**
Assessment 2 relates to my instructional goals by…	___ I drew upon my knowledge of language instruction to design instructional strategies appropriate for, and tightly connected to, the instructional goals and individual student needs.
The assessment was appropriate for Student A because…	
The assessment was appropriate for Student B because…	

(*Continued*)

Copyright material from Erin E. H. Austin and Lisa Bartels (2026), *Achieving National Board Certification in World Languages*, Routledge

TABLE 7.1 (*Cont.*)

Student A's assessment results show me they were struggling with… I know this because…	___ I analyzed assessment results. ___ I examined my students' individual needs in relation to the lesson at hand and to long-term objectives.
Student B's assessment results show me they were struggling with… I know this because…	
The results of the assessment impacted my subsequent teaching because…	___ I made adjustments to curriculum and instruction consistent with my findings on the assessment.
I built on my students' progress after this assessment by…	___ I examined my students' individual needs in relation to the lesson at hand and to long-term objectives.

(*Continued*)

TABLE 7.1 (*Cont.*)

Sentence starters from the prompts: Reflection	Checklist of the most applicable rubric points
Some things in this instructional sequence that worked well for my two students' learning were… ♦ ♦ ♦ After each bullet, provide specific examples and data on why it worked well.	___ I accurately describe my own practice. ___ I analyze my practice fully and thoughtfully, and reflect on its implications and significance for future practice.
One thing that did not work as well as I expected was… because… To improve this in the future I will…	
Some ways I used resources/technology in this lesson were: ♦ ♦ ♦	___ I adapted, created, and used appropriate resources to meet the needs of all my students.

(*Continued*)

TABLE 7.1 (*Cont.*)

One time I changed my plans during class was…	___ I accurately describe my own practice.
because (tell what happened to prompt the change)…	___ I analyze my practice fully and thoughtfully, and reflect on its implications and significance for future practice.
I changed plans because of (cite your knowledge of language acquisition to justify the change)…	
Note: You may repeat this box for more additional changes to your original plan.	
I would/would not change my assessment strategies because…	
I would/would not change the type of feedback I provided because…	

(*Continued*)

TABLE 7.1 (*Cont.*)

My assessment results showed me I met Student A's needs and encouraged their learning because… (Give specific examples from the assessment.)	___ I fostered creative and critical thinking among my students. ___ I examined my students' individual needs in relation to the lesson at hand and to long-term objectives.
My assessment results showed me I met Student B's needs and encouraged their learning because… (Give specific examples from the assessment.)	

"Component 2 Instructions and Scoring Rubric," National Board for Professional Teaching Standards 7–9, 14)

This table is downloadable from the Routledge webpage for this book, which can be found here: resourcecentre.routledge.com/books/9781041205357.)

Back to the Beginning

How do you solve a problem like Maria (had)? There's no question Maria is an effective teacher, her students love her, and their summative performance brought the audience to (joyful) tears! She also used a variety of techniques. Kurt's activity was for practicing vocabulary, and Brigitta's activity was focused on culture. Every student did every activity. This is all excellent! However, her approach doesn't meet the C2 criteria, which requires differentiation, not simply "doing different stuff during class."

The solution is for Maria to provide Kurt and Brigitta with *different* activities for learning the *same* vocabulary. This could involve stations where students choose from several practice activities, 1:1 instruction, or another method. She could follow this with *different* activities for Kurt and Brigitta to learn the *same* cultural point. For example, she could provide different articles (on the same culture) based on reading level, or she could have some students listen to the audio while reading and others read silently to themselves. Thus, Kurt and Brigitta would receive *differentiated* instruction to achieve the *same* goals. This change of approach would give Maria *confidence in sunshine, confidence in rain,* and confidence that her C2 portfolio shows accomplished teaching!

(Note: If you're missing our reference here, please stop writing and *immediately* go watch *The Sound of Music*! You cannot be accomplished in *life* without it. Humble opinion.)

References

National Board for Professional Teaching Standards. *Early Adolescence through Young Adulthood/World Languages: Component 2 — Differentiation in Instruction.* Prepared by Pearson under contract with the National Board for Professional Teaching Standards, © 2021, *National Board for Professional Teaching Standards*, https://www.nbpts.org/certification/candidate-center/first-time-and-returning-candidate-resources/#candidate-instructions. Accessed 7 Aug. 2025.

8

Component 3

Teaching Practice and Learning Environment

Mr. Schneebly wanted his C3 video to stand out, so he chose a game show format complete with theme song and flashing lights. In his best announcer voice, he read questions aloud in Spanish. Students had 30 seconds to write down and "lock in" their answers on individual whiteboards; correct answers got an applause sound effect while wrong ones got a sad trombone. The kids were 100% engaged and could be heard on the video talking about how much fun they were having. Best of all, by the end of class Mr. Schneebly documented that every student was answering the questions with 90% accuracy … and Mr. Schneebly discovered a possible retirement career as a game show host!

Confident his lesson was creative, engaging, and effective, Mr. Schneebly eagerly awaited his NBPTS results. Unfortunately, there were no fireworks, leaving him discouraged and confused.

Summary of Component 3

Component 3 (C3) focuses on instructional design and delivery. Using two 10-to-15-minute videos of their classroom, candidates illustrate how they skillfully design and deliver lessons to students. The two videos show different lesson formats and instructional goals, painting an overall picture of candidates' accomplished classroom practice. The C3 rubrics focus heavily on high-level instructional practices such as selecting quality resources; fostering student engagement, collaboration, and inquiry; equipping students with language learning skills; and improving target language communication ("Component 3 Portfolio Instructions and Scoring Rubric," National Board for Professional Teaching Standards 13, 18). Close attention to the rubrics is crucial as you design and implement your lessons, because not all good lessons will meet the rubric requirements. (Definitely read that last sentence again. And again.)

What You Will Turn In

Your C3 portfolio will include a one-page Introduction to Entry form. Additionally, for *each* video, you will submit up to eleven written pages:

- Instructional Context Form (one page)
- One 10-to-15-minute video file
- Instructional Planning Form (one page)
- Written description of your instructional planning (up to two pages)
- Instructional materials for the lesson (up to three pages)
- Written Commentary (up to four pages)

The entire portfolio entry will include up to 23 pages of written materials and two video files.

Accomplished Portfolios

According to the C3 rubrics, we believe assessors are looking for evidence that you:

- Make intentional decisions at each point of your lesson.
- Base decisions on evidence from your students and on your masterful understanding of language acquisition.
- Set appropriate goals for students.

- Design instruction to effectively meet those goals for *all* students.
- Select high-quality, appropriate, authentic instructional materials.
- Foster communication *with* students and *among* students in the target language.
- Encourage student inquiry and language learning strategies.
- Incorporate target culture(s).
- Adapt instruction and provide appropriate feedback based on student needs.
- Skillfully articulate your thinking at each step of instruction. (C3 instructions, 18)

Planning Your Entry: Choosing Your C3 Lessons

As you contemplate which lessons to film for C3, consider these factors:

- Your selected lesson should respond to students' needs, based on data and evidence about your class. (Refer to Chapter 4 for a refresher on demonstrating Knowledge of Students.)
- Your two videos should show the breadth of your teaching ability. You may use the same group of students for both videos, and some candidates have no choice! If you are able to record different classes, this can demonstrate your ability to adapt for different proficiency levels. Either way, your two videos should show different teaching formats (e.g., direct instruction, partners, group work, games, student choice, stations) and different instructional goals. Think outside the box! What formats do you use that are unique or especially engaging? How do you teach different modes of communication? Use your pair of videos to showcase your ability to flex for different instructional demands.
- Your videos do not have to show a high level of student proficiency nor perfect results. Rather, they must illustrate

how you craft instructional experiences to meet students' needs and to move them into deeper levels of proficiency.
- ♦ The C3 rubrics look for high-level skills. Review them in detail, and think about how to demonstrate the student-centered elements in your lesson (18).

 **Your Turn!**

Brainstorm lessons you might video for C3. What are the format and goals of each lesson, and what needs will it address?

Possible Class and lesson to video

Format and goals for this lesson:

Student needs this lesson will meet, and notes about what I want to highlight:

Possible Class and lesson to video

Format and goals for this lesson:

Student needs this lesson will meet, and notes about what I want to highlight:

Possible Class and lesson to video

Format and goals for this lesson:

Student needs this lesson will meet, and notes about what I want to highlight:

Showcase Your Theory: Planning Your C3 Lesson

Like other written components, C3 begins with a deep analysis of your students. You must show you know the students *well* and have combined this knowledge with your expert understanding of language instruction to set one or two appropriate goals for this class. As always, we recommend choosing at least one proficiency-based goal, as this provides more depth and opportunity for analysis. This might be a good time to review the suggestions in Chapter 4 regarding Knowledge of Students and in Chapter 7 (C2) related to Goal Setting. Carefully selecting goals for your specific class that are well-supported by strong pedagogy is the bedrock of C3.

Your next step is planning your lesson. You'll want to thoughtfully curate each activity *and* each resource to move students closer to your goal, reflecting your very best lesson design. There are days when time gets away from us and we use activities from someone else—and that's OK. We *all* do it! But don't underplan *this* lesson! This is your "A game." The C3 rubrics look for evidence that you "skillfully use authentic, culturally appropriate, rich, and thought-provoking instructional resources and realia to engage students in developing communicative skills in the target language." (See what a mouthful that is? And that's just *one* of the rubric points! That's why it's important to read the rubrics as you plan!) Don't forget to consider current best practices regarding authentic target culture resources, and plan how you will support students in interpreting those sources. (See Chapter 2 for more discussion of authentic resources.) In your Written Commentary, you will explain your choice of instructional materials, so document your rationale for choosing each resource. While not required by NBPTS, it is to your advantage to do something creative, innovative, or out-of-the-box. You want assessors to finish reading your portfolio and think, "What a great idea! I want to try that in my classroom!" As we advised in Chapter 2, this is not a place to play it safe!

If all that isn't enough, your featured C3 lessons should also show students engaging in challenging tasks and interacting with each other in the target language. This, of course, is more difficult than direct teaching or supervising independent work—and that's the point! Most teachers can stand in front of the class and deliver information, but accomplished language instructors foster student inquiry, productive struggle, and target language use. To keep you on your toes, you never really know how this type of lesson is going to work out when you add students to your plan! Accomplished practitioners design a solid lesson and then react flexibly to meet student needs during class.

One question we hear a lot is, "How much target language should I use?" The answer: This is up to your professional judgment. (Just what you wanted to hear, right?) NBPTS provides no guidance regarding the amount of English used in class. The critical factor is your analysis of *why* you used English vs. the target language, and that the choice of language is intentional and appropriate for your instructional purpose. Keep in mind that the C3 rubrics evaluate your effectiveness in fostering *student* target language communication. It may be difficult to score well if your videos do not show the students using some target language (with intelligible audio!).

Showcase Your Practice: Capturing Your Videos

For anyone not born with a portable recording device attached to their hand (shoutout to Gen X!), recording video may not be intuitive, so it's important to think through the logistics of capturing your C3 videos. The C3 instructions do not call for slick production; they just ask for videos showing you and your students interacting with intelligible audio. Capturing clear sound is probably the trickiest (and the most important) aspect of recording your C3 lessons, so experiment with different setups. Having a colleague follow you with the camera may yield great sound quality, but it might add to the already-present existential dread of speaking in your poor little cherubs! Students already think you're nerdy, so going all-in and wearing a lapel mic or using a tabletop conference mic are options. For the under-thirties in our readership, your phone probably does a great job of capturing sound (which you already know from TikTok). With those options in mind, we recommend you experiment with different AV arrangements in your empty classroom before recording with students. If your school has a media specialist, they can probably help!

While you can (and should) have a clear plan for how your video lesson will go, you need to maintain some flexibility on the direction of your entry until your video clips are captured. The C3 instructions assume you will make strategic instructional decisions *during* the lesson, and the prompts ask for thoughtful analysis of what actually happens in the videos.

No matter how well you plan, at least two factors (other than your own tech-challenged or tech-savvy generational distinction) can prevent you from capturing amazing videos for C3. First, you never know for sure how students will respond to your instruction. Second, students are often very nervous about being recorded and may react either by clamming up *or* by hamming up for your video! (One of the authors had to throw out a recording because, as she leaned over to help a student, kids behind her were nudging each other and flipping off the camera. Oh, teenagers ... we love you.) To mitigate these hiccups, we recommend you record several lessons as you prepare your C3 entry. Some teachers even set up a camera in their classroom for days ahead of their featured lesson. This gets students used to being recorded, it allows you to troubleshoot technical issues (especially sound), and it gives you many videos to choose from, which makes student antics a lot easier to laugh at! By having your camera as a semi-permanent classroom fixture, your students may not even realize when they are or aren't being recorded, resulting in more natural classroom interactions. If you only record one lesson, on the other hand, you are stuck with whatever happens for better or worse.

Showcasing Your Practice: Video Analysis

Once you have a few videos to choose from, take time to watch them! Are there visible instances of students interacting in the target language, engaging in inquiry, and/or of you providing feedback that would convincingly illustrate your expertise? On the other hand, are there visibly disengaged students, lots of off-task behaviors, or mischievous "flying birds" in the background? *That's* not what you want to show! In our experiences recording video for NBC, we have been frequently surprised; our impression of "how it's going" during a lesson is not necessarily representative of what shows up on the recording. A video clip may capture a great student conversation you weren't aware of, highlight a problem during instruction that you took steps to solve, or illustrate productive student struggle. Remember what Forrest Gump (kind of) said: Your videos are like a box of chocolates; you never know what you're going to get!

✎ Your Turn!

As you watch your videos, note moments that support C3 rubric points and might therefore provide rich content for analysis. Aim to demonstrate every point between your two videos.

TABLE 8.1 Chart to analyze your recorded lesson

Evidence assessors are looking for (adapted from the C3 rubrics) (18)	Evidence from my video that supports these criteria (video number, timestamp, and short description)
The learning environment is *safe, fair, equitable*, and *challenging*, based on trust and mutual respect. *Note: Address all four adjectives.*	Video #___ Timestamp _____ Description:
The lesson includes self-directed learning, active student engagement with the teacher *and* other students, sharing ideas, conversing purposefully, and/or listening attentively during activities. *Note: Show engagement with the teacher and with other students.*	Video #___ Timestamp _____ Description:
Students explore topics of substance *and* use an inquiry process. *Note: Show both.*	Video #___ Timestamp _____ Description:
Students communicate and collaborate in the target language with skills such as asking thoughtful questions, responding respectfully to others' ideas, building consensus, compromising, negotiating, and accepting ambiguity. *Note: We recommend you show evidence of at least three of these skills.*	Video #___ Timestamp _____ Description:

(*Continued*)

TABLE 8.1 (*Cont.*)

The teacher provides regular constructive feedback to students.	Video #____ Timestamp _____ Description:
The teacher supports *all* students in advancing their speaking, listening, reading, and writing abilities in the target language so that they can engage in meaningful and culturally appropriate communication. *Note: Discuss how you support all students. We recommend illustrating at least two of the four modes of communication in your pair of videos.*	Video #____ Timestamp _____ Description:

"Component 3 Instructions and Scoring Rubric," National Board for Professional Teaching Standards 18. (This table is downloadable from the Routledge webpage for this book, which can be found here: resourcecentre.routledge.com/books/9781041205357.)

As you write, be sure to analyze more than you describe. Assessors can see what happened in your video, so you don't need to spill a lot of ink describing long sequences of classroom activity. Instead, give assessors a window into your thinking during lesson delivery. You can use phrases like "When the girl in the red shirt said X, I responded Y because I know..." "At timestamp A, B happened. This showed me ... So I..." Keep your description of events just brief enough to let assessors know what you're referring to; the bulk of your entry should explain *why* you took particular actions during the lesson.

Explain your decision making in detail. Did you take steps to ensure every student had supplies? To scaffold activities from easy to more difficult? To differentiate for individual learners? To informally assess student understanding as you taught? To individualize feedback based on your knowledge of each student? As teachers, we incorporate these and many other practices intuitively, but you cannot expect assessors to make assumptions about your rationale for what they see in the video. In fact, it is likely your assessors will read your commentary first, evaluate whether your analysis is clear, consistent, and convincing, and only *then* watch your video for confirmation. Therefore, your written commentary must make your intuition visible, even on actions that seem really obvious to you. It may be helpful to think of what you would tell a student teacher about the actions you took in your video. A colleague or mentor who watches your video might also help you articulate practices you performed intuitively.

Here's an example: Mrs. Baker customizes her questions so students of different ability levels can be successful. For closed-answer questions (e.g., yes/no, this/that), she calls on struggling students, sometimes after verifying they have written the right answer. This gives a higher probability for success to build upon. For more confident students, she provides open-ended questions or asks for on-the-spot modifications to learned content. She also is acutely aware that who is struggling and who is confident can vary from day to day.

Mrs. Baker has done this for so long, she doesn't even realize when she's doing it and certainly doesn't write it into her lesson plan. However, this practice shows Mrs. Baker knows her students well and modifies instruction in real time to meet their needs. In her C3 Commentary, Mrs. Baker should write about why she uses this approach, citing specific examples from her video.

 Your Turn!

What practices do you do intuitively, and why do you do them? Do you see examples of these practices in your videos, and how could you incorporate them into your C3 Commentary?

What instructional practices do I do intuitively?

Why do I do these things?

Where is it present in my videos?

Case Study Practice

Based on this chapter, what significant error did each candidate make?

Example 1: Ms. Darbus captured an amazing video. However, she struggled with the page limit on her Written Commentary; she didn't really have space to write out everything that happened in the video.

Ms. Darbus' Error:

Example 2: Miss Beadle arranged for a friend to come in and record class on March 16 during third and fourth periods (for her two videos). That way, she will be able to write her entry during spring break.
Miss Beadle's Error:

Example 3: Señora Hill scaffolded her lesson carefully to introduce a concept and guide students to begin using it. In her Written Commentary, she explained how excited the kids were when they progressed through each step of the lesson and mentioned how one student became a lot more confident as a result of the activity.
Señora Hill's Error:

Example 4: Ms. Gruwell gave students a short Spanish story to read. If students had trouble, they could look up words online. After reading the story, students answered questions on a worksheet. Then Ms. Gruwell went through the right answers, and students corrected their worksheets before turning them in.
Ms. Gruwell's Error:

Example 5: Mr. Morgan recorded an activity where students used their phones to scan QR codes. Two students didn't have phones, so Mr. Morgan told them to pair up with a student who did have a phone.
Mr. Morgan's Error:

Example 6: Miss Clavel had students watch a video in English that was made by an NY-based tour company promoting travel to Morocco. Then students talked about Morocco compared to their home culture. At the end of the lesson, Miss Clavel told the students some of the words they used in French.
Miss Clavel's Error:

Example 7: Mr. Kenobi is under a time crunch to complete C3. He finished most of his Written Commentary and then watched his video to make sure he didn't miss anything. Some of the kids are goofing around in the video (one even said "This is soooo boring!") but hey—kids will be kids, right?
Mr. Kenobi's Error:

Example 8: Mrs. Mason's outstanding lesson speaks for itself! To make sure assessors don't miss it, she writes, "At the end of the video you can see how effective the lesson was!"
Mrs. Mason's Error:

 ## Case Study Analysis

Let's look at where each teacher went wrong.

Example 1: It sounds like Ms. Darbus has fallen into the common trap of describing rather than analyzing her lesson. Instead of "writing out everything" from her video, she should highlight how key moments illustrate her thinking before, during, and after instruction.

Example 2: I hope Miss Beadle's kids are on their A-game March 16 and there's no fire drill, flu outbreak, Spring hormones, or weather delay! She's stuck with whatever happens in class that day ... unless she arranges for a few more video sessions before the (rapidly approaching) submission deadline.

Example 3: Señora Hill designed and delivered a successful lesson, but she didn't explain why and how she achieved these amazing results. She needs to put what's in her head down on the paper, rather than describing student reactions that assessors can see for themselves.

Example 4: There's nothing particularly wrong with Ms. Gruwell's lesson, but it's also not very innovative. It's unclear whether students are really communicating in the target language, and little evidence that Ms. Gruwell's feedback is effective. Ms. Gruwell needs to ensure her lesson provides convincing evidence of the C3 rubric criteria.

Example 5: Two of Mr. Morgan's students do not have resources to complete the lesson and must rely on peers. This is not equitable! Mr. Morgan needs to design instruction and/or seek out resources so all students have the same access.

Example 6: None of Miss Clavel's instructional resources are authentic, and there is no target language communication taking place. While there may be a place for this type of lesson, Miss Clavel's C3 portfolio is probably not that place. She needs to carefully review the C3 rubrics and design a lesson to demonstrate those criteria.

Example 7: It's too bad Mr. Kenobi put in so much work before watching his video, which will almost always show activities the teacher wasn't aware of during instruction. In this case, the video illustrates some lack of engagement—exactly what you don't want to show in C3. Mr. Kenobi would be wise to find the time to record another (more engaging) lesson.

Example 8: Mrs. Mason may be correct that her lesson had an impact. Unfortunately, assessors can't read her mind. She needs to explicitly state what the impact was and how she knows.

Remember, C3 is all about your teaching practice and learning environment. Your lessons do not have to go *perfectly*, but they should go *well*! Your videos are case studies which you use to illustrate your thought process in creating a student-centered, communicative classroom.

Common Pitfalls

As you develop your C3 portfolio, be alert to these common errors:

- Failure to show "meaningful, interesting, and comprehensible activities." Your C3 lessons should represent your top teaching, not an ordinary or ho-hum lesson. Refer back to the "Should I Take a Risk or Play It Safe?" section in Chapter 2.
- Not showing student-centered activities. Review the C3 rubrics carefully; the bar is high. Successful submissions demonstrate many soft skills related to language learning, and successful candidates showcase these elements.
- Choosing low-quality instructional resources. The C3 rubric asks candidates to justify their choice of materials as "authentic, culturally appropriate, rich, and thought-provoking" (9). That's a lot!
- A focus on outcome over process. The goal of C3 is *not* to demonstrate high student achievement, but to demonstrate your thinking in coaching students toward improvement. This is very different from most teacher evaluations we experience in our job.
- Lack of flexibility. Show assessors how you adapted to unexpected moments during instruction and how each decision moved students a little closer to the goal.
- Not showing much target language use. You don't have to be 100% in the target language, but you *do* need to show how you foster target language communication among your students.
- Not mentioning good things you did. Candidates commonly fail to articulate solid pedagogical practices like

selecting appropriate resources, effective questioning, making input comprehensible, differentiating, scaffolding, modeling, etc. Assessors can't make inferences about your rationale for what you did; they can only score what you actually write.
- Describing more than analyzing. To reference something from the video, a quick mention with a time stamp is all you need. The analysis that comes after it is more important. Most of your Written Commentary should tell how and why you planned as you did.
- Low-quality sound. *You* might know what your students said, but if the assessor can't hear it, they can't score it. It may be worth giving your video to a friend, colleague, or unsuspecting family member and asking, "Can you hear everyone clearly?"

Drafting Your Written Commentary

After carefully planning your lesson and capturing a convincing video, it's time to start writing. These sentence starters, adapted from the C3 instructions, are a good starting point. Later, revisit what you've written and confirm it meets the criteria on the right, adapted from the C3 rubrics. Remember, if you don't write it, assessors can't evaluate it.

You will complete the charts below separately for *both* of your videos.

TABLE 8.2 Sentence starters and C3 rubric checklist

Sentence starters from the prompts | Writing about planning (with the Instructional Context Sheet: up to two pages)	Checklist drawn directly from the most applicable NBPTS C3 rubric points (Please refer to the rubrics for precise wording, and also note the rubrics are holistic, so many points overlap with multiple prompts.)
My knowledge of my students' _____ influenced my planning and choice of strategies because… *(fill in the blank with a word of your choice: backgrounds/needs/abilities/interests.)* (Repeat with two or three more of the words above.)	___ I draw on detailed knowledge of students' backgrounds, needs, abilities, and interests, and on my own knowledge of world language learning.
My knowledge of world language learning influenced my planning and choice of strategies because…	
These are the instructional challenges represented by my students:	
The social and physical context I described influenced my planning by…	

(Continued)

Copyright material from Erin E. H. Austin and Lisa Bartels (2026), *Achieving National Board Certification in World Languages*, Routledge

TABLE 8.2 (*Cont.*)

My long-term goals (for this school year) for these students are:	___ I select high, worthwhile, and attainable goals.
These goals are appropriate for these students because…	
I chose this instructional format to meet the goals of this lesson because…	___ I select instructional approaches and instructional resources that support these goals. ___ I provide students with meaningful, interesting, and comprehensible activities that are connected to the learning goals, and sequence and structure instruction so that students can achieve the goals.
I selected these instructional resources for this lesson because… *Note: You may want to borrow language from the rubrics regarding your resources being authentic, culturally appropriate, etc., as you answer this prompt.*	___ I skillfully use authentic, culturally appropriate, rich, and thought-provoking instructional resources and realia to engage students in developing communicative skills in the target language.

(*Continued*)

TABLE 8.2 (*Cont.*)

Sentence starters from the prompts | **Written Commentary** (up to four pages) *Note: Wherever possible, cite proof or examples directly from your videos to illustrate your analysis.*	Checklist of the most applicable rubric points
The pedagogical and instructional decisions I made during the lesson aligned with/differed from my planning in these ways:	___ I create a student-centered learning environment based on trust and mutual respect. ___ I facilitate the inquiry process. ___ I equip students with skills that support communication and collaboration in the target language, such as the ability to ask thoughtful questions, respond respectfully to others' ideas, build consensus, compromise, negotiate, and accept ambiguity.
I used _____ (specific approach/ technique/strategy/activity) to promote student engagement. This is evident in the video when… because… (Repeat this prompt for more examples.)	___ I promote self-directed learning and active student engagement with me and other students in sharing ideas, conversing purposefully, and listening attentively during activities as students explore topics of substance. ___ I support all students in developing the proficiencies necessary to advance their speaking, listening, reading, and writing abilities in the target language so that they can engage in meaningful and culturally appropriate communication.

(*Continued*)

Copyright material from Erin E. H. Austin and Lisa Bartels (2026), *Achieving National Board Certification in World Languages*, Routledge

TABLE 8.2 (*Cont.*)

I established a safe learning environment for all students by…	___ I have established a safe, fair, equitable, and challenging environment.
I established a fair learning environment for all students by…	
I established an equitable learning environment for all students by…	
I established a challenging learning environment for all students by…	
I monitored and assessed student progress during the lesson by…	___ I monitor and evaluate student learning.
My monitoring and assessment influenced my decision making during instruction by… *Note: This refers to decisions made* during instruction *that weren't necessarily part of your plan.*	___ I make instructional adjustments as part of an ongoing process of assessment.

(*Continued*)

TABLE 8.2 (*Cont.*)

I provided student feedback by…	___ I provide regular constructive feedback to students.
I provided it in this manner because…	
I *fully/partially (etc.)* achieved my goal for this lesson because…	___ I communicate persuasively about the pedagogical decisions made before, during, and after instruction.
This is evident in the video when… because…	___ I describe my practice accurately and analyzes it fully and thoughtfully.
My next steps with these students will be… because…	
My past experience influenced how I taught this content to the students in this video because…	

(*Continued*)

Copyright material from Erin E. H. Austin and Lisa Bartels (2026), *Achieving National Board Certification in World Languages*, Routledge

TABLE 8.2 (*Cont.*)

One thing I would do differently if teaching this lesson to a similar group again is… because… OR I would not change anything if teaching this lesson to a similar group again because… (*Note: We recommend you share a maximum or one or two tweaks to make your very successful lesson even better next time.*)	___ I reflect insightfully on implications of classroom impact for future teaching. ___ I strategically seek ways to improve my practice to promote student learning.

"Component 3 Instructions and Scoring Rubric," National Board for Professional Teaching Standards 11-12, 18). (This table is downloadable from the Routledge webpage for this book, which can be found here: resourcecentre.routledge.com/books/9781041205357.)

Back to the Beginning

Remember Mr. Schneebly's amazing game show lesson? It was fun, effective, and had lots of bells and whistles (literally). Unfortunately, the lesson doesn't really address many of the points in the C3 rubrics. There are no authentic resources, no self-directed learning, no feedback beyond "right or wrong," and not much student target language use. Therefore, even though his lesson is clearly effective, Mr. Schneebly received a low score on C3. To avoid this fate, read and re-read the rubrics, plan your lessons to meet their criteria, take multiple videos, and work to foster the depth of student engagement NBPTS requires. Close attention to the rubrics, coupled with social media-worthy video clips, will help your submission stand out in all the *required* ways!

References

National Board for Professional Teaching Standards. *Early Adolescence through Young Adulthood/World Languages: Component 3 — Teaching Practice and Learning Environment.* Prepared by Pearson under contract with the National Board for Professional Teaching Standards, © 2021, *National Board for Professional Teaching Standards,* July 2017, https://www.nbpts.org/certification/candidate-center/first-time-and-returning-candidate-resources/#candidate-instructions. Accessed 7 Aug. 2025.

9

Component 4

Effective and Reflective Practitioner

Working on Component 4 (C4) inspired Ms. Frizzle to develop one of the best units of her career! After working with her school art teacher to create lessons about target culture artists, Ms. Frizzle collected donations of art supplies from the community. Then, students created their own target culture-inspired paintings, which were displayed at a local art gallery. This collaboration was amazing! The gallery featured her students' work at a formal gala, which was attended by parents, school administration, and local dignitaries. Local news even broadcast a story about the project, which Ms. Frizzle was proud to include as C4 evidence.

Months later, Ms. Frizzle received her NBC results. She was shocked; her C4 entry scored very poorly. How could this be? Her unit was pure magic! Unfortunately, Ms. Frizzle's experience is not uncommon. How did she miss the mark?

Summary of Component 4

C4 is unique among NBC entries, as it primarily evaluates the candidate's decision-making process and ability to improve their own practice, rather than student outcomes. There are several parts to C4, and it may help to think of them as "mini-components" in a larger portfolio showcasing your accomplished practice. As you address each requirement, you will paint an overall picture of your approach to gathering and acting on data for your students' benefit.

What You Will Turn In

The submission requirements for C4 are more complex than the other portfolio entries. (Some candidates enjoy naming it. Might we suggest, "The Beast," "The Black Hole," or "The Soulcrusher"? You can watch a Monster Truck rally for inspiration.) So please refer attentively to the C4 submission guidelines. Be careful to organize and plan evidence to meet these requirements:

- Contextual Information Form (one page)
- Group Information and Profile Form with supporting evidence (up to four pages)
- Instructional Context Form (one page)
- Formative Assessment Materials Form, with information about the assessment, the results, and student reflections (up to nine pages)
- Summative Assessment Materials Form, with information about the assessment and its results (up to five pages)
- Description of Professional Need Form with supporting evidence (up to three pages)
- Description of Student Need Form with supporting evidence (up to three pages)
- Written Commentary (up to twelve pages)

As you can see, you may submit up to 38 pages for C4. Only 12 of those pages are Written Commentary. In other words, the forms and accompanying evidence are integral to your C4 portfolio, and each artifact should be selected intentionally. Ready or not, here comes each element of C4 in detail!

Accomplished Portfolios

According to the Component 4 Portfolio Instructions and Scoring Rubric (National Board for Professional Teaching

Standards 25), we believe assessors are looking for evidence that you can:

- Collaborate with many stakeholders to develop a deep understanding of a class.
- Recognize trends in a group of students and factors that may impact those trends.
- Design effective assessments and insightfully interpret assessment results.
- Guide students in conducting meaningful self-assessment.
- Set strategic goals for your own professional growth.
- Participate in professional development and/or collaboration that directly benefits your students. This collaboration may or may not be related to world language content.
- Seek out resources to develop your own teaching practice.
- Identify a student need requiring your involvement beyond the classroom through "advocacy, collaboration, and/or leadership."
- Access and incorporate a variety of resources to meet your students' needs.

Easy, right? (Insert sarcasm here.) C4 is full of little pieces. The common thread is a focus on your *process* for improving your own instruction. The idea is to show how you use data to identify needs in your students and in your own teaching, and how you then draw from a wide range of resources to meet those needs. This process should directly impact your own students and may extend beyond your classroom.

There are two broad sections to C4. For the first section, you will showcase one unit, from beginning to end, in one of your classes. The focus here is how you use formative, summative, and student self-assessment to help kids improve. The second section of C4 involves selecting a professional need *you* have and a need *your students* have. You will write about how you used a variety of resources to meet those needs, resulting in improved student performance. Take a moment to brainstorm what you might feature for the two parts of C4; as you learn more, you may come back and make adjustments!

✎ Your Turn!

Brainstorm some possible topics for C4 requirements.

Possible Units to feature assessment and student self-analysis:

Possible professional needs (related or unrelated to course content) from the past two years:

Possible student needs that require your advocacy beyond the classroom from the past two years:

Part 1: Showcase your Theory and Practice with Knowledge of Students

Like C2 and C3, C4 begins with a deep dive into your students, this time for an entire rostered class. Start by reviewing Chapter 4 of this book, and develop a thorough knowledge of one of your classes. The C4 instructions stipulate that you use "multiple sources" to develop your class profile and suggest these possibilities: assessment or school data, observational data, information from parents and caregivers, and community characteristics. We recommend you include *at least* one source of information from each suggested category and connect it to your group's classroom performance. This information will drive your eventual portfolio focus. You can begin collecting data, and perhaps even writing the group profile section of your commentary, before you develop the rest of your C4 portfolio.

✎ Your Turn!

What information will you describe in your Group Information and Profile form?

Choose several information sources from this list, adapted from the (C4 instructions, page 8)

- Student assessment data from previous years
- Other school data
- Observational data
- Information from families and caregivers
- Information from school personnel who have worked with these students or a similar group of students
- Community factors that may influence these students

Information I collected:

How I collected it:

I know _____ about this group of learners because:

I need more information about _____ because: *(Note: If you identify an area where you need more information, be sure to address how you found the info and what you did with it later in your entry.)*

Some other important factors about this group are:

These factors influenced my planning and decision making by...

Selecting Supporting Documentation for Your Class Profile

For each section of C4, you'll provide either two or three pages of supporting documentation. NBPTS has some suggestions for this! They recommend including at least two examples of "progress charting, email records, ongoing notes, (and) other appropriate methods of sharing information" (9). These artifacts are important! In fact, assessors are likely to review this supporting documentation before they begin reading your Written Commentary. You'll want to make sure your selected information aligns with and reinforces what you write.

For your class profile, look for several examples of data from different sources that all tell the same story. You will need to explain your rationale for selecting and prioritizing your data sources, so think carefully about the "why" for each decision you make. The instructions do not simply ask for quantity or variety of data, so copying a lot of facts onto the page is not enough. This section is your chance to prove your ability to synthesize data from many sources and to draw insightful conclusions about how to help this specific group of students.

As you develop your Knowledge of Students, be on the lookout for great quotes, anecdotes, or data you might ultimately include in these supporting documentation pages. The C4 instructions ask you to "label evidence appropriately" (16), and you can use these labels to your advantage. A phrase such as, "chart showing student improvement in ____" or "quotes from students about ____" can help your assessors quickly understand the story you are telling through your selection of each artifact.

Your Turn!

What trends do you see in your group, and why?

Trend in this group of students

    Based on this data (include more than one source):

    Rationale for including each of these sources:

    Possible artifact(s):

Trend in this group of students

    Based on this data (include more than one source):

    Rationale for including each of these sources:

    Possible artifact(s):

Trend in this group of students

> Based on this data (include more than one source):

> Rationale for including each of these sources:

> Possible artifact(s):

Part 2: Showcase your Theory and Practice with Generation and Use of Assessment Data

Now that you've dissected your guinea pig class, it's time to turn the microscope on your process of gathering and using information to plan your teaching. It won't surprise you to learn the C4 rubrics set the bar high: they ask you to show you understand that "assessment is a recursive process that involves setting initial learning goals, administering assessments that are appropriate to measure students' progress toward those goals, evaluating student progress … and setting new learning goals to improve student learning" (26). Like always, that's a *lot*. Let's look at each element one at a time to make it less intimidating.

Setting Learning Goals

The C4 instructions ask you to reference your "unit objectives" as you describe your planning for these students, but there is no guidance about how to choose them. Fear not! *We* have guidance:

- ♦ The overarching goal for C4 is to demonstrate your ability to collect, analyze, and use data to improve student outcomes. Like every step in the NBC process, your

goals should be curated for these students, based on their unique needs and your professionalism.
- ♦ A proficiency-based objective gives more opportunity to showcase accomplished practice than a purely content-based objective. For example, the proficiency-based goal "Students will be able to speak about a past event" requires deeper learning than the content-focused goal "Students will be able to conjugate preterite verbs". For a deeper look at setting proficiency-based goals, refer to Chapter 7.
- ♦ Part of C4 involves your ability to foster student self-assessment. Keep this in mind as you choose objectives. If you can select a goal students are excited about or have themselves identified as a need, this can inspire better student self-analysis…which they're not naturally great at! (For real. You need to help them. More on this later…)
- ♦ Go deep, not broad. One or two unit objectives is plenty. If you choose more, you're looking at a lot of sleepless nights ahead.

Administering Appropriate Assessments and Selecting Supporting Documentation

Your next step is gathering data through a formative (or pre-teaching) assessment to document what students can already do. Design or select your formative assessment thoughtfully! Whether you use a pre-made assessment or create your own, your goal is to pinpoint exactly what your students can do related to your objectives and to determine their next steps. What questions will help you better understand this class? What assessment format will be most effective? Remember, you are not limited to a traditional paper-and-pencil test. Projects, verbal assignments, activities, or graphic products could provide useful evidence. In your Written Commentary, you will justify your assessment design, so be sure your choices are intentional and tightly aligned to your learning goals for this group.

✎ Your Turn!

Prepare to administer your formative assessment.

Unit objective(s):

Data I need about my students' current ability:

Questions or assessment format I will use to get that data:

Why this assessment is appropriate, consistent, fair, and accurate: *(Note: this is from the instructions (page 14). Address all four adjectives).*

In C4, you will submit your assessment or a description of your assessment along with up to two pages of results. Try to feature results that show students really *do* need to improve in the objective you've chosen. (You know when you're reading student work and can tell right away they don't know anything, and their answer is a total stretch? Assessors can tell when adults do this too!)

In your Written Commentary, you will reference these examples and show how they directly influenced your lesson planning. This is an important place to demonstrate your decision-making process; everything should be aligned. This is also a great place to think about additional resources or collaborations (with families, colleagues, or community members) that could help students achieve your objectives.

 **Your Turn!**

Select and use supporting documentation from your formative assessment results.

>Specific artifacts to include as evidence from my formative assessment results:

>What this evidence tells me about my students:

>How this knowledge will impact my planned instruction:

>Additional resources or collaborations that may help:

As you teach, do your plans change (before or during instruction?) Why? Who helped you on your journey of improvement? Keep track of all of this; you're going to write about it later! (Post-Its! Post-Its everywhere!)

Evaluating Student Progress: Student Self-Assessment

There is only one prompt in C4 regarding student self-assessment and use of feedback; however, this topic comprises two of the nine bullet points on the rubric (i.e., over 20% of the rubric!) (C4 instructions, pages 14, 25). In other words, fostering self-assessment and reflection is easy to overlook, but neglecting this major element of C4 is a critical mistake! No pressure!

Students do not typically self-assess naturally or well, and many toss the teacher's carefully crafted feedback in the trash without ever looking at it! (Or is that just *our* students?) What does this mean for your NBC portfolio? You have to take time to intentionally teach self-assessment and reflection. Here are a few practices that may spark your thinking:

- Teach and use self-assessment *before* you begin your featured C4 lesson. This will give your students practice at self-assessment and will give you practice coaching them. It also lets you troubleshoot the process before collecting the reflections you *need* for your portfolio.
- Use rubrics. Simplify the language in rubrics so it is meaningful to students.
- Coach students in setting their own learning goals and developing rubrics or checklists to match them.
- Ask students to evaluate both good and bad examples of sample work against the rubric; then ask them to reflect on how their own work compares to those samples.
- Give students exit tickets or self-reflection activities, and hold them accountable to give more thoughtful answers than "IDK." Consider prompts like: "The best part of my work was...", "One thing I want to improve is...", "I am proud of...", and "I still have questions about..." (each followed by *"because..."*).
- Hold conferences or coaching sessions to discuss progress with students.

Those are some ways to demonstrate that you "help students become active participants in their education and to evaluate and think critically about their performance." (C4 instructions, page 25). As students reflect on their formative assessment results, don't forget to collect the suggested three pages of self-assessment materials for your portfolio. Ideally, the student reflections will add another layer of evidence showing all the steps of your featured unit are integrated.

 **Your Turn!**

Consider how you will foster student self-assessment.

Self-assessment technique:

    Questions or prompts:

    How you will support students to reflect meaningfully:

Self-assessment technique:

    Questions or prompts:

    How you will support students to reflect meaningfully:

Self-assessment technique:

    Questions or prompts:

    How you will support students to reflect meaningfully:

Evaluating Student Progress: Your Summative Assessment

The process for developing your summative assessment is similar to that of the formative assessment and should provide measurable evidence of student growth through the unit. What assessment format and questions or tasks will provide you with direct evidence regarding your students' performance? The goal is to show assessors you know how to design an assessment that is tightly aligned to your objectives and that you draw insightful conclusions from the results.

 **Your Turn!**

Brainstorm some possible features of your summative assessment.

Unit objective(s):

Data I need about my students' current ability:

Questions or assessment format I will use to get that data:

Why this assessment is appropriate, fair, consistent, and accurate: *(Note: this is from the rubric. Address all four adjectives).*

This is where you can really shine! Show how your students have made measurable progress toward your goal(s). Of course, this is thanks to your accomplished teaching! You will share your assessment or a description of it, along with two pages of assessment results, in your summative assessment documentation. Feature results that illustrate your students' *progress* and also show logical next steps in this group's learning journey.

Setting New Goals

You're almost done with the assessment part of C4! The remaining piece is easy: Using examples from the data you shared, plan your students' next steps. By identifying and justifying one or two new objectives, you demonstrate your understanding of the continuous cycle: goals -> instruction -> assessment -> analysis of data -> new goals.

 **Your Turn!**

Analyze your summative assessment results.

> Specific evidence from my summative assessment results to include in my portfolio:

> What does this evidence tell me about my students' progress?

> What trends or patterns are present?

> Possible next steps specifically based on these results:

✎ Your Turn!

Now that you've thought through your assessment design, how will you describe the following elements on your Formative Assessment Materials form and Summative Assessment Materials Form? (Note: The instructions on p.9 say to *describe*)

Formative Assessment

Describe the assessment you used:

Describe how the assessment aligns with your teaching objectives:

Describe how the assessment results support your teaching practice:

Why is this assessment appropriate for this group of students?

How did you develop or select this assessment?

How did you administer and score this assessment?

How do you intend to use the results of this assessment?

Summative Assessment

Describe the assessment you used:

Describe how the assessment aligns with your teaching objectives:

Describe how the assessment results support your teaching practice:

Why is this assessment appropriate for this group of students?

How did you develop or select this assessment?

How did you administer and score this assessment?

How do you intend to use the results of this assessment?

Common Pitfalls for Parts 1–2

As you develop your portfolio, take care to avoid these common C4 pitfalls:

- Failing to show cause and effect. Every sentence in your writing should fit into this cycle:

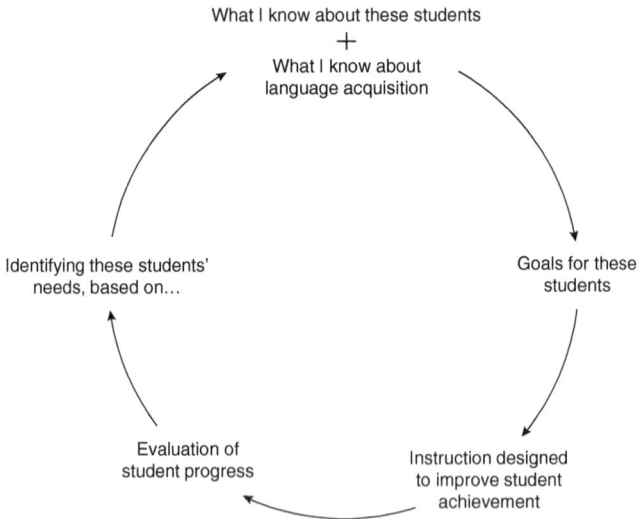

FIGURE 9.1 The Instructional Cycle

- Providing lots of data, but not connecting it to student achievement or to your decisions as an educator. Numerous disjointed facts aren't enough; they need to tell a story about this class.
- Using canned curriculum. While you are allowed to use pre-made curriculum, show you evaluated it and possibly modified it to meet these specific students' needs. Writing something like, "This is the next test in Spanish 2," shows you can *follow* directions, but not that you are an accomplished practitioner who *sets* the direction of your class. If you are required to use certain assessments, see our advice in Chapter 7.
- Choosing objectives that are too basic or closed-ended. Help your students develop proficiency.
- Underplanning and/or underteaching student self-assessment. Most kids don't know how to do this; it's up to you to show them!
- Underdeveloping the student self-assessment portion of C4. The C4 rubric weighs student self-assessment and use of feedback more heavily than the prompts might suggest. Plus, the C4 instructions call for three pages of supporting documentation for student self-assessment. It's a big deal on the rubric, so don't gloss over it.

Case Study Practice

Using the guidance in this chapter, what significant errors did each of these teachers make in their C4 design?

Example 1: Miss Geist gave a pretest where students completed five listening activities on an online platform and printed out their results. She reflected that the students really struggled with this activity, and several kids did not complete it. Miss Geist is planning to have students do worksheets and games to build their vocabulary before they listen to the online platform again for their summative assessment.

Miss Geist's Error:

Example 2: Mr. Hall asked students to do reflections on their writing assignments. He was happy that a lot of students wrote, "I did my best" and "I think I did good." Mr. Hall used these quotes as evidence that his students are building confidence in their writing.
Mr. Hall's Error:

Example 3: For his summative assessment, Mr. White gave a test where students had to write the correct verb conjugation for different sentences.
Mr. White's Error:

Example 4: Ms. Teagues wanted to impress assessors, so she shared three results from her top students who all got "A's" on the test.
Ms. Teague's Error:

 ## Case Study Analysis

Let's examine each teacher's error.

Example 1: Miss Geist's observation that students "struggled with listening" is probably true, but how does she know, and what will she do about it? Will the worksheets and games she has planned actually help students improve their listening proficiency? Will she have data to prove it? Miss Geist needs to explain a clear progression from the assessment results to her instructional plans based on sound pedagogy.

Example 2: The three most common student self-assessment responses are probably "I did good," "(insert unrelated drawing here)," and "IDK." Predictably, NBPTS is looking for something deeper: evidence students can identify their own strengths and weaknesses, set goals, and take ownership in developing proficiency. Since that doesn't sound like Mr. Hall's students, he will have to coach them in thoughtful reflection. He should consider introducing a rubric, checklist, or similar system for students to routinely evaluate their own progress.

Example 3: Mr. White's choice of a verb conjugation test doesn't provide much information. Proficiency, proficiency, proficiency!

Example 4: Ms. Teagues is rightfully proud of her high-fliers! But did these students show growth (or need her help at all)? C4 is about your process in developing your students—not necessarily their perfect results. This may be easier to show with students who have more room for growth or who have specific challenges and need your expertise.

For more information about successful assessment design, see Chapter 7 (Component 2).

Whew! Congratulations on absorbing the information on the first two parts of C4. You're on your way! If you are ready to start drafting Parts 1 and 2 of your Written Commentary, you can jump to the workbook prompts at the end of this chapter. On the other hand, if you'd like to tackle Parts 3 and 4, read on. There are also ideas for blending the parts of C4 later in this chapter, if you're leaning toward that approach. They can be written separately or as a whole, so choose your own adventure!

Part 3: Participation in Learning Communities

In Part 3 of C4, you will select two needs: a professional learning need of yours *and* a need of a group of students. Please note:

- You should select both needs based on evidence and your knowledge of students.
- The two needs may be related or unrelated to the other parts of your C4 entry.

- ♦ The two needs may be related or unrelated to each other.
- ♦ The two needs can be related to your content area but do not have to be. You can use other types of needs (e.g., Social-Emotional, basic academic skills, training in a particular area or technique, resources in your classroom, school, or community).
- ♦ Your professional need must require collaboration.
- ♦ Your student needs must require "advocacy, collaboration, and/or leadership on your part" (12).
- ♦ Both needs must be "clearly connected to student learning and your practice" (12).

Let's say this part together with slow claps: These needs are based on my knowledge of students and my strong pedagogy, and meeting them will improve student learning.

Choosing Your Own Professional Learning Need

For your own professional learning need, think of a problem you have encountered and solved (or want to solve) in your practice. How did you identify this need? What made you seek out a solution, and who helped you? Some possible sources of collaboration include:

- ♦ Formal training
- ♦ Colleagues in any role
- ♦ Educational Specialists outside the school (e.g., district staff, the PTA, professional organizations)
- ♦ Parents and caregivers
- ♦ Student organizations
- ♦ Community resources
- ♦ Fundraisers or Grants
- ♦ Sharing your learning beyond your classroom

Remember, you are not collaborating for collaboration's sake. Like everything else in NBC, your goal is to show how student learning improved, either directly or indirectly, through your efforts.

✏️ Your Turn!

Brainstorm some possible needs and collaborations.

    Possible professional learning need:

    Evidence that this is a need (list multiple sources):

    Possible collaborations to meet this need and why:

    How this collaboration could improve student learning:

    Possible professional learning need:

    Evidence that this is a need (list multiple sources):

    Possible collaborations to meet this need and why:

How this collaboration could improve student learning:

The C4 instructions have only one (multi-part) prompt for the professional and the student needs, so the "Description of Need" Forms and evidence are key. This is your chance to show off what you did and how you know it had an impact. Choose wisely! A certificate of attendance at a professional development workshop, for example, does not prove students learned anything. Better evidence could be a screenshot of slides you developed from that workshop, before and after scores, or student testimonials about your epic class!

Choosing Your Student Need

Like your professional need, tackle your student need by thinking about past events in your classroom or school. What have you noticed about students in the past 12 to 24 months? What concerns you? What would you like to change to improve learning? Remember, this need can be academic or non-academic, and it can impact your own students, your entire department or school, colleagues, or the broader community. In other words, you have wide latitude in choosing your student need. The one non-negotiable is (let's say it one more time, all together!): You must show how your work impacted student learning in the 12 months prior to the portfolio submission window opening!

Some ideas for addressing a student need include:

- Improving academic performance through a new instructional technique or initiative
- Improving study skills, social-emotional growth, mental health, or other soft skills
- Improving attendance or access to school resources
- Conducting outreach to a special population

- Procuring resources
- Mentoring, tutoring, or other academic support
- Holding clubs or cultural initiatives
- Developing school-community partnerships
- Teaching or training programs
- Advocacy at any level
- My idea: _____

Select artifacts from the 12 months prior to the submission window opening that document impact on students, such as data showing improved student outcomes, testimonials, products created due to your initiative or documented results of your work. Evidence can be quantitative or qualitative and can show direct or indirect student impact. Good notes will help you write about the impact of your efforts in your Written Commentary.

 Your Turn!

Brainstorm some possible student needs for your C4 portfolio.

Possible student need with supporting data:

How I could provide advocacy, collaboration, and/or leadership:

Possible evidence to show impact on student learning:

Possible student need with supporting data:

How I could provide advocacy, collaboration, and/or leadership:

Possible evidence to show impact on student learning:

Common Pitfalls for Part 3

Lots of candidates fall into these traps. Don't let this happen to you!

- Providing evidence without a clear purpose. This error can happen at any point in the portfolio; candidates may provide a smorgasbord of unrelated artifacts for any of the C4 forms. Data on its own isn't enough. You must show how you *interpret* and *use* this data to help your students grow.
- Choosing a need for yourself or your students without explaining *why* the need should be addressed and *how you know*.
- Failing to draw a connection between the need you identified and your action steps. You must align these elements.
- Failing to show how your efforts impacted student learning. You are not trying to prove you completed professional learning or collaboration just for fun; your purpose is always student growth.

❓ Case Study Practice

Using the guidance in this chapter, what significant errors did each of these teachers make in their C4 design?

Example 1: Mrs. Krabappel is concerned that enrollment in French classes has declined for four consecutive years. For her Professional Learning Need, she selected the goal of "making French class more fun."
Mrs. Krabappel's Error:

Example 2: Coach Bolton believes students would do better in school if their parents were more involved. He organizes several events for parents to visit their students in class and also gives them tours of the school in Spanish.
Coach Bolton's Error:

Example 3: As evidence of meeting her Professional Learning Need, Professor Sprout. (make that Dr. Sprout!) provided a screenshot of her college transcript and a photo wearing her new yellow and black doctoral regalia.
Dr. Sprout's Error:

Example 4: Mr. Garvey brought in a guest speaker who grew up in Peru. He also collaborated with a local restaurant to donate Peruvian food for his students to try. As artifacts, he included photos of the guest speaker and a copy of the restaurant menu. Kids loved it!
Mr. Garvey's Error:

Case Study Analysis

Let's examine how each teacher could strengthen their portfolio.

> **Example 1:** Mrs. Krabappel has identified a need and has some data to justify it. However, she doesn't explain how this need connects to her goal of "making class more fun." Additionally, this goal is very general, and it is unclear how it will improve learning.
>
> **Example 2:** Coach Bolton may be correct about the need for parent involvement. However, he needs to incorporate data and evidence showing how he knows this is a need, how it will improve learning for these students, and why he has designed this specific outreach to meet the need.
>
> **Example 3:** Earning a doctorate is a huge milestone! Unfortunately, unless Dr. Sprout shows evidence that her learning impacted students, her achievement may not lead to National Board Certification.
>
> **Example 4:** Mr. Garvey has described a successful classroom experience, but he has not analyzed it. What student need was he addressing? Why did he choose these collaborations? What is his evidence that the activities improved student learning? Mr. Garvey needs to carefully answer the C4 prompts, rather than just describing a lesson he is excited about.

Each of these teachers is doing great things for students! Unfortunately, the C4 rubrics don't measure how fun your class is; they measure your decision-making process. Each of these teachers failed to show a link from student need to their actions to results. We feel this is a common reason for low scores on C4.

Ideas for Blending Parts 1, 2, and 3

Now that you know what the first three parts of C4 are all about and how you could deal with them individually, let's look at how they might be integrated. If you already have a plan for writing them individually, go for it! You can skip this part! However, blending the three parts can make your job easier because much of the evidence you collect about your featured class could apply to your entire entry. This can give you a cohesive theme to write about, making it easier to justify your choice of professional and student needs.

How do you choose a theme to weave through the entire C4 entry? One approach is to start with your own professional development (PD). Think of impactful PD you have completed in the past two years. Why did you seek out this specific PD, and how did that experience help you meet your students' needs? How are you currently applying it in your featured class? If you have clear answers to these questions, that topic could be a great starting point for C4.

Another technique to integrate your entry is identifying a particular academic need that you don't yet know how to address. Seeking out a solution to this problem and applying it in your featured class could give your portfolio cohesion.

Please bear in mind that some candidates blend the elements of their portfolio, while others address the parts separately. Either approach is acceptable, so long as you show your accomplished practice in evaluating and using data in each area to benefit your students.

Your Turn!

If you would like to integrate your portfolio topic, capture your thinking here.

Possible portfolio theme

Unit of instruction related to this theme:

Professional need related to this theme:

Student need related to this theme:

Possible portfolio theme

Unit of instruction related to this theme:

Professional need related to this theme:

Student need related to this theme:

The last step of your C4 Written Commentary is a reflection on your use of data. Review the Reflection section in Chapter 4 to create a convincing and professional conclusion to your portfolio.

Drafting Your Written Commentary

These sentence starters, adapted from NBPTS C4 prompts, can help you draft your written commentary. Including phrases like, "I know X about my students/about teaching my target language, so I…" or "When I saw Y, I decided to…because…" will help assessors understand your rationale for each action you took. When you finish, check your work against the rubric points on the right.

TABLE 9.1 Sentence starters and C4 rubric checklist

Sentence starters from C4 prompts | Knowledge of Students Suggested length: 2 pages	Checklist drawn directly from the most applicable points on the NBPTS C4 rubrics (Please refer to the rubrics for precise wording, and also note the rubrics are holistic, so many points overlap with multiple prompts.)
I gathered information about my students from these sources:	___ I collaborate effectively with families and caregivers, colleagues, and others to develop information about a group of students.
These considerations guided me in selecting these particular sources of information:	
These sources were appropriate for the information I was gathering about these students because…	___ I insightfully evaluate the information for relevance and relative importance. ___ I collect, analyze, and compare data skillfully to identify trends and patterns.
I determined the relative importance of the information I gathered by… *Note: This is an easy point to overlook*	
I identified these trends from the information I gathered:	

(*Continued*)

TABLE 9.1 (*Cont.*)

I confirmed the trends by…	
Some other factors I took into account when analyzing and reflecting on these sources of information were… because…	
Based on my analysis, my class needs…	___ I apply the in-depth knowledge gathered about the group of students in planning effective and fair instruction. ___ I use collected information to design, instruction to meet students' needs. ___ I understand that assessment is a recursive process that involves setting initial learning goals…
I anticipate providing these supports to meet my students' needs in fair and equitable ways:	
I will need to collaborate with these people to meet my students' needs: because…	___ I apply the in-depth knowledge gathered about the group of students in planning effective and fair instruction. ___ I methodically expand my own professional knowledge through collaborations with families and caregivers, colleagues, the community, or other learning communities in order to contribute measurably to student learning and growth.

(*Continued*)

Copyright material from Erin E. H. Austin and Lisa Bartels (2026), *Achieving National Board Certification in World Languages*, Routledge

TABLE 9.1 (*Cont.*)

Sentence starters from the prompts | Generation and Use of Assessment Data Suggested length: 5 pages	Checklist of the most applicable points from the rubrics
This is how the knowledge I developed about my students AND my unit objectives influenced the kinds of assessments I planned to use:	___ I apply the in-depth knowledge gathered about the group of students in planning effective and fair instruction and assessment. ___ I collect, analyze, and compare data skillfully to design, evaluate, and modify assessment practices to meet students' needs.
This is how the knowledge I developed about my students AND my unit objectives influenced the modifications I needed to make to assessments: (e.g., modifications for students' learning modalities, social-emotional growth, exceptionalities, interests)	___ I understand that assessment is a recursive process that involves administering assessments that are appropriate to measure students' progress toward the goals I set to improve student learning.
I took these steps to ensure my assessment results gave consistent, fair, and accurate information about student performance:	___ I select or create assessments that measure what I intend to measure.

(*Continued*)

TABLE 9.1 (*Cont.*)

My analysis of formative assessment results showed me this about my class's performance in relation to unit objectives:	___ I understand how to use assessments for formative purposes to gain information about student progress. ___ I collect, analyze, and compare data skillfully to identify trends and patterns and use that information to design, evaluate, and modify instruction and assessment practices to meet students' needs.
I saw these patterns, trends, and outliers in my formative assessment results: Pattern or trend #1: Specific example(s) from submitted evidence: Pattern or trend #2: Specific example(s) from submitted evidence: Outlier: Specific example(s) from submitted evidence:	
I also considered these factors as I analyzed formative assessment results: because…	

(*Continued*)

Copyright material from Erin E. H. Austin and Lisa Bartels (2026), *Achieving National Board Certification in World Languages*, Routledge

TABLE 9.1 (*Cont.*)

I made these changes to my unit plans based on formative assessment data:	___ I understand how to use assessments for formative purposes to gain information about student progress and to inform and modify instruction.
Specific data from formative assessment:	___ I collect, analyze, and compare data skillfully and use that information to design, evaluate, and modify instruction to meet students' needs.
Action based on this information:	
because…	
Specific data from formative assessment:	
Action based on this information:	
because…	

(*Continued*)

TABLE 9.1 (*Cont.*)

Based on formative assessment results, I provided these additional resources or supports: because…	
Based on formative assessment results, I took these steps to collaborate with others: because…	___ I methodically expand my own professional knowledge through collaborations with families and caregivers, colleagues, the community, or other learning communities, in order to contribute measurably to student learning and growth.
My analysis of summative assessment results showed me this about my class's performance in relation to unit objectives:	___ I understand how to use assessments for summative purposes to gain information about student progress. ___ I understand that assessment is a recursive process that involves setting new learning goals to improve student learning based on the analysis of summative assessment results and knowledge of students. ___ I collect, analyze, and compare data skillfully to meet students' needs.

(*Continued*)

Copyright material from Erin E. H. Austin and Lisa Bartels (2026), *Achieving National Board Certification in World Languages*, Routledge

TABLE 9.1 (*Cont.*)

I saw these patterns, trends, and outliers in my summative assessment results: Pattern or trend: Specific example(s) from submitted evidence: Pattern or trend: Specific example(s) from submitted evidence: Outlier: Specific example(s) from submitted evidence:	
Summative assessment results inform my plans going forward by… because…	

(*Continued*)

TABLE 9.1 (*Cont.*)

I also considered these factors as I analyzed summative assessment results: because…	
I supported students in using the feedback from unit assessments by… This helped students achieve unit objectives because… *Note: This question does not appear in the NBPTS C4 instructions, but it addresses the rubric point on the right.*	___ I help students effectively apply feedback from assessments in ways that positively impact the students' learning.
I supported student use of self-assessment in this unit by… This helped students achieve unit objectives because…	___ I actively encourage, guide, and support student self-assessment to help students become active participants in their education and to evaluate and think critically about their performance.

(*Continued*)

TABLE 9.1 (*Cont.*)

I will apply the knowledge I accumulated about this class and the assessment results in future instruction in these ways:	___ I understand that assessment is a recursive process that involves evaluating student progress and setting new learning goals to improve student learning based on the analysis of results and knowledge of students.
Specific information about this class:	___ I apply the in-depth knowledge gathered about the group of students in planning effective and fair instruction and assessment.
How it will impact future instruction:	
Specific information about this class:	
How it will impact future instruction:	
Sentence starters from the prompts | Participation in Learning Communities **Suggested length: 2 pages**	**Checklist of the most applicable points from the rubrics**
I identified my need for professional learning by…	___ I systematically and insightfully reflect on ways to improve my instructional and assessment practices that will lead to improvements in student learning and growth.

(*Continued*)

TABLE 9.1 (*Cont.*)

I considered these factors in determining how to meet that need: because…	
Meeting this need impacted student learning in these ways:	___ I methodically expand my own professional knowledge by participating in professional development. ___ My activities contribute measurably to student learning and growth.
I identified the student need requiring my advocacy, collaboration, and/or leadership by…	
I worked with… and my role was…	
I considered these factors when determining how to meet the student need: because…	

(*Continued*)

TABLE 9.1 (*Cont.*)

The need was *schoolwide/content-specific* (choose one and explain) Addressing this need impacted student learning in these ways:	___ My activities contribute measurably to student learning and growth.
Sentence starters from the prompts | Reflection **Suggested length: 3 pages**	**Checklist of the most applicable points from the rubrics**
I know my efforts to develop knowledge about this group of students were effective because… *Note: Focus on how your efforts led to improved student learning outcomes.*	___ I systematically and insightfully reflect on ways to improve my instructional and assessment practices that will lead to improvements in student learning and growth
In the future, I might take these different approaches or additional steps to develop knowledge of students: because… *Note: We recommend you suggest one small improvement here.*	

(*Continued*)

TABLE 9.1 (*Cont.*)

My assessment practices have evolved… (*complete at least one of these prompts*) ♦ as I gained knowledge of my students by… ♦ as I learned from my experiences by… ♦ as I interacted with others by… ♦ as I participated in professional development or learning communities by…	
My professional learning and collaborative activities *were/were not* as effective in improving student learning as I expected because of these factors: *Note: We recommend you highlight why your activities were largely effective, with a maximum of one idea to make it even better next time. Remember to focus on student learning outcomes.*	

(*Continued*)

TABLE 9.1 (*Cont.*)

What is your plan to continue impacting student learning in the future? (*Complete at least one of these prompts, or address them holistically.*) ♦ I will develop knowledge of students to impact student learning by… ♦ I will collaborate with others to impact student learning by… ♦ I will use assessment to impact student learning by… ♦ I will participate in learning communities to impact student learning by… ♦ Overall, as a result of my activities in C4 I will continue impacting students by…	

"Component 4 Instructions and Scoring Rubric," National Board for Professional Teaching Standards 14-15, 24. (This table is downloadable from the Routledge webpage for this book, which can be found here: resourcecentre.routledge.com/books/9781041205357.)

Back to the Beginning

Remember Ms. Frizzle and her amazing art unit? She was so confused about her low C4 score when she clearly did such amazing things for students. The answer lies in two phrases in the C4 rubric:

"The portfolio provides clear, consistent, and convincing evidence the candidate:

- collaborates…to develop information about a group of students *and insightfully evaluates the information for relevance and relative importance.*
- methodically expands his/her own professional knowledge…*in order to contribute measurably to student learning and growth*" (emphasis added).

Do you see what The Frizz missed? Although she described an exceptional unit, she didn't provide evidence of her analytical skills related to student needs and student learning. Fortunately, you now have the tools to avoid this error as you demonstrate your accomplished use of data to drive your decisions and improve student learning.

References

National Board for Professional Teaching Standards. *Early Adolescence through Young Adulthood/World Languages: Component 4 — Effective and Reflective Practitioner.* Prepared by Pearson under contract with the National Board for Professional Teaching Standards, © 2021, *National Board for Professional Teaching Standards,* https://www.nbpts.org/certification/candidate-center/first-time-and-returning-candidate-resources/#candidate-instructions. Accessed 7 Aug. 2025.

SECTION 3
What's Next?

10

After Submitting Your Portfolio

At this point, you've taken your language proficiency tests (OPI, WPT), taken your C1 test, and submitted portfolios for C2–C4. Congratulations! That's a monumental feat in and of itself, and you should absolutely be proud of your accomplishments because it *is* a big deal! While you're waiting for results, we hope you do something celebratory that makes you happy. You deserve it.

The problem, however, is now you're at the point plenty of candidates feel is the toughest step yet: waiting for results! Will the oft-discussed NBPTS fireworks await you … or not *yet*? No matter where you fall, there are "next steps" to consider.

No Fireworks: Next Steps

First—and we cannot stress this point enough—this is a *process*. If you venture into each component submission knowing that you put forth your best work possible *to date*, yet also not *expecting* a passing score, you're doing yourself a favor. Historically, a sizable percentage of candidates don't pass every component the first time through. In fact, the most influential teacher Erin ever had didn't pass on the first time through … and she missed it by a soul-crushing .06 points.

DOI: 10.4324/9781003716860-13

Despite both receiving *overall* passing scores on their first time through, Erin and Lisa each had a piece of the portfolio whose results were less than desirable:

Erin: C4 is my nemesis! As I was working on it and not-so-affectionately calling it "The Beast," I knew it was a significant hurdle to sort through the multiple parts of C4. It felt so much bigger than the others, but ultimately, I thought I found a solid focus and had done worthwhile work for myself and my students. Then I got my score report. Boy, was I off! I bombed C4. Fortunately for me, Lisa knocked C4 out of the park, so as we've dissected the NBC process together, I see what I did wrong: I did good work, but I didn't do what I was asked to do. Namely, my cause and effect weren't as tight as they should have been and my analysis wasn't strong, mainly because I was tired and coasting on previous high scores!

Lisa: My weakest—and my strongest—scores were both on the C1 constructed responses. Like most candidates, I did what I could to prepare for the test, and when I arrived at the testing center, I was focused, determined … and nervous! When each constructed response question came up, I took a few minutes to outline my response and then typed like my fingers were on fire! I was happy with my submissions and felt I'd represented myself well. When the scores came out, I was both happy and sad. One of my constructed responses had an amazing score … and one was a complete bomb. I have no idea why! (Did I read the prompt wrong? Write in English when it should have been French? Was my answer just that terrible?) These questions still bug me to this day. Letting go has never been my strong suit. My results weren't perfect, I don't know why, and that's okay.

If a similar tale happens to you, you're not the only one; *it's common*. Breathe and reboot. *It doesn't mean you're a bad teacher.* Here are our top five tips to move you forward:

1. Solicit useful feedback. As previously mentioned, the only ("canned") feedback that NBPTS assessors are allowed to give is not especially helpful. Therefore, if

you don't understand what went wrong after reading this book, give your submission to someone who is familiar with the process and who can look through it and give you personalized feedback. Choose someone who isn't afraid to give constructive criticism; conversely, make sure you're *ready to hear* constructive criticism. If your problem area was C2–C4, this is simple. However, if your problem area was C1, this will take the form of a conversation since you won't have a hard or electronic copy of your work to give to anyone.

2. Don't beat yourself up. *Oodles* of wonderful teachers don't score high on any given component the first time through, so it's a mistake to correlate a low score with poor teaching. Not always, but *often*, it's not a matter of how they taught but a matter of how they chose to write about it. We recommend re-reading Chapters 3 and 5 to help with this specific issue.

3. Consult the NBPTS scoring calculator. This is on the NBPTS's website, and it's there to support candidates in developing a retake strategy. Keep in mind that C1 and C3 are weighted more heavily than C2 and C4, so some candidates feel like retaking C1 and/or C3 will result in better "bang for their buck." One of the best qualities of C1 is that it's done in a single day, but another fine attribute is that if you don't do as well as you would like, you can retake only *part* of the component. Whew!

4. Lean on others for support. This is an excellent time to re-read this book, to find a mentor, and/or to join an online or in-person community of world language educators working together on NBC. It's remarkable how much the simple act of going through a difficult process in a community setting makes the load feel lighter.

5. Carefully consider timing. NBPTS releases score reports in December, so it can be a fast turnaround to make a decision, re-register, pay for a component, do the work,

and submit again the following May. This is especially true if you choose to redo C4, which is more complex. If you know right away what you can improve, this may not be a problem. However, if you feel as though you're starting from scratch, a worthwhile approach might be to spend a year planning and doing the work. Then re-register the *following* school year, as long as you still meet the timing requirements for your scores to remain valid.

Finally, you may be simply asking yourself, "Should I even continue?" If that's where you find yourself *today*, you're not alone, although it's wise to leave some space and time for a change of heart. In the end, there is not one right way to work through this process.

We are also acutely aware that cost can be prohibitive for would-be NBCTs. Cost notwithstanding, if you're close to reaching the minimum weighted scaled score, which at the time of this publication is 110, we recommend going for it!

But after completing the entire portfolio, if your weighted scaled score is still far from the minimum required score, you feel exhausted from the process, and the idea of redoing all or close to everything is too daunting, give yourself permission to stop if that's what feels most right. Everyone reading (and writing!) this book has had experiences that didn't turn out the way they planned or hoped, and there's something to be said for channeling your inner Dr. Ross Geller and *pivoting*. This is akin to when high school students spend years building up skills for an AP or IB exam and don't pass. That score doesn't take away from the fact that they learned valuable skills in the process, skills that can't be taken away or discredited ... and we tell them that, now don't we? Simply by undertaking this work for any amount of time, you have proven that you are committed to improving your teaching. Your pivot might be considering what new step is out there for you that will also improve your teaching. Pick something that sounds interesting, and then go out there and get it! We're cheering you on from beyond these pages!

Fireworks: Next Steps

Whether it's on your first time through or after your umpteenth attempt, fireworks are fireworks, and you *passed!* Congratulations! You're likely feeling a delightful little mix of pride, joy, relief, and total exhaustion, and you're not alone. Take time away from everything NBPTS-related and *rest*. Bask in the feeling of having earned certification. Ahhh…

When you're ready, we recommend doing two things. First, go through everything you have that's related to your professional life and put "NBCT" after your name: on business cards, in your email signature, and in your bio on your school's website. It will feel glorious! Second, contemplate the answer to, "What now?" The more NBCTs you know, the more a clear pattern emerges: By and large, NBCTs are go-getters who continually strive for improvement.

So what, then, is on the horizon for you? What is your next move? Here are our top five ideas to get you started:

1. Advocate! As of this publication, the NBPTS is only certifying teachers in two world languages: Spanish and French. We'd like to see this changed … *yesterday*. However, it won't change without our advocacy, so contact the NBPTS directly (e.g., calls, emails) and indirectly (e.g., tagging the NBPTS in social media posts). Urge other NBCTs to do the same and to do it regularly!
2. Advocate *more*! Now that you're an NBCT, it's time to advocate for all NBCTs on the building, district, state, and national levels. Check to see if your state is one of the many with social media groups where NBCTs band together, discuss advocacy work, and encourage leadership (at various levels) to recognize and reward this distinction.
3. Pay it forward. Think of a friend or colleague who might enjoy and/or benefit from the NBC process and encourage that person to check it out. Be up front with the workload (or feel their wrath later!), but also share ways candidates can find the support needed to succeed.

4. Network with other NBCTs. Either virtually or in person, networking with other NBCTs can be rewarding and professionally enhancing.

> **A personal note from Erin:** I will never forget the first time I encountered NBCTs en masse. I was a class of 2018 Global Learning Fellow with the NEA Foundation, and nearly every state was represented in our group. Over the course of a year, we spent considerable time together in online webinars and in person in Washington D.C. and South Africa. During this time, I noticed something right away: This group of teachers, more than any group I'd ever been around—including being raised in a family of educators and working in a variety of school settings—was overwhelmingly positive. I hate to admit this, but teachers can be incredibly negative, spending time when we're together focusing on everything that's not going well in our particular contexts. This group of fellows, however, was wonderfully different. These teachers were passionate and excited about the multitude of cool things they were doing professionally, in the classroom and outside of it. They shared stories and ideas, resources and contacts. They worked together to innovate. Did they say everything at their schools was perfect? Not by a long shot; there were certainly problems. But the prominent features of the interactions were joy and innovation. "What's with this group?" I wondered. These fellows had vastly different settings and lives from my own and from each other, but there was a common thread: A striking number of them were NBCTs. "Hmm," I thought. "Maybe there's something to this…" and it was during that year that I started my own journey to becoming a NBCT.

NBCTs innovate and lead. And it's infectious! Networking with other NBCTs can do wonders to strengthen your classroom practice or, if you're looking for a shift, open other doors in the education sphere.
5. Be a joiner. If you haven't already, now is an excellent time to join a professional organization. Nationwide, we have seen NBCTs creating forward progress as members of organizations and in positions of leadership. Use your knowledge and expertise to affect positive development for students and teachers.

No matter where your NBC journey happens to be at this moment, know that there are still steps in this process. Reach out to others, create community, and make a difference for yourself and for students.

11

Maintenance of Certification

NBC is like training for a big race. It takes effort, endurance, and maybe a few tears. You might even get sick on the side of the road! When you finally cross that finish line, you're exhausted but satisfied. You know you've earned it.

However, this big race is just one milestone on a lifelong journey of wellness. You did so much work, and you want to maintain your gains. Do you still have to eat well? Spend time in the gym? Get up early to exercise? Yes, yes, and yes. But it's not as hard. You've put in the work, and now it's routine.

Introducing: Maintenance of Certification (MoC)! MoC is simply your training; it's keeping your career "fit" and not letting all the hard work from initial certification atrophy. It won't be as hard as initial certification, but it does require a high level of instructional "fitness." It's showing the world you've remained strong as an educator and leader.

Maintenance of Certification Summary

To maintain NBCT status, you will complete Maintenance of Certification every five years ("Maintenance of Certification," National Board for Professional Teaching Standards 1). Since you have already demonstrated to NBPTS that you are an accomplished teacher, you no longer need to "prove yourself." Rather, MoC documents how you have maintained your high level of accomplished teaching and continue to positively impact

DOI: 10.4324/9781003716860-14

student learning. MoC can be completed much more quickly (and cheaply!) than your original NBC portfolio, and the vast majority of MoC candidates successfully maintain certification.

The MoC submission is divided into two components. In Component 1, you will analyze how you continued to support student learning over the past five years through two Professional Growth Experiences (PGEs). In Component 2, you will analyze a classroom video showing one of your PGEs in action (NBPTS 2–3). The overarching goal of your portfolio is to demonstrate continued growth as an educator and positive impact on student learning since your last NBPTS achievement.

What You Will Turn In

Component 1 requires:

- A Written Commentary about your two PGEs (cover sheet, prompt page, and up to eight pages of your content)
- Supporting documentation, referred to as "Samples of Product," showing impact on students (cover sheet and up to two pages of documentation per PGE/five total pages)
- If applicable, translations of your supporting documents (for languages other than English or your TL; translations do not count in your page total)

Component 2 requires:

- A video recording of a lesson demonstrating one PGE (up to 10 minutes)
- A Written Commentary (cover page, prompt page, and up to five pages of your content)

MoC FAQs

This chapter is less intense than the others in this book…and with good reason! The MoC instructions provide quite a lot of guidance for candidates, including advice for choosing your

PGEs (MoC instructions, pages 5–7), writing tips (MoC instructions, pages 39–41), and useful charts (MoC instructions, pages 33–35) to help plan your entry. The MoC rubric is much simpler than the rubrics for initial NBC—thank goodness! As a result, this chapter will not duplicate any of that information. So here is the same advice we all give our students: *Read the instructions!*

(suspenseful music plays)

Now that you've read and absorbed the MoC instructions, you may still want some guidance. These are the most common questions we hear when working with MoC candidates.

Q: Is X a good PGE?

A. Usually, the answer is "yes." Good PGEs meet these criteria:

- ◆ You selected the PGE because of a need related to education. The need can be as narrow as one student or as broad as your school, community, nation, or entire profession.
- ◆ The PGE resulted in you growing professionally.
- ◆ Student learning improved, either directly or indirectly, through your work.

Most worthwhile professional activities will meet these criteria; your challenge is to analyze and write convincingly about the experience. See Chapter 3 for tips on writing for NBPTS.

Q: One of my PGEs is not related to teaching language. Is this OK?

A. Probably, yes. One of your PGEs needs to lend itself to filming a lesson about your target language. The other PGE can be almost anything! (Anything related to education, that is! It might be hard to justify a PGE beach trip, even though a few days in the sun might indirectly improve your classroom instruction!) The MoC instructions ask you to improve your content and/or pedagogical knowledge (MoC instructions, page 2). It's fine for one of your PGEs to focus on broader pedagogy, as long as your efforts improve student outcomes.

Q: **I've moved into a new position and no longer teach language. What should I do?**

A: Congratulations! Hopefully you are changing the world in your new role! You can choose almost anything for one PGE, but you need to film a language lesson for the other one. Find your most exhausted colleague and offer to teach their class to complete this requirement. Remember, you still need to demonstrate Knowledge of Students, so you might want to visit the class several times (and possibly film more than one lesson) as you work on MoC.

Q: **What should I include as Samples of Product?**

A: The goal is to show impact on students. This impact can be direct or indirect, quantitative or qualitative. Good evidence could include student work samples, before and after student data, support or instructional materials you developed as part of your PGE, or impact statements from anyone you worked with. There are no formatting requirements for MoC, but common sense dictates materials should be a legible size. For a more detailed discussion about choosing effective supporting documents, see Chapter 9.

Q: **How do I capture good video?**

A: Video recording can be one of the biggest challenges for MoC—but we've got your back! Please refer to Chapter 8 for a detailed discussion of all things video.

Q: **What are assessors looking for?**

A: Based on the MoC rubric, we believe assessors want to see evidence that:

- You identify needs and take action to meet them.
- You have continued to grow as a teacher.
- Your work has a positive impact on student learning.

All of these answers go back to the Architecture of Accomplished teaching (see Chapter 2). Keep doing what you're doing, and think of MoC as a chance to document your amazing work!

Common Pitfalls

Most MoC candidates are successful, but be alert to these pitfalls:

- Lacking deep knowledge of your students. This is most common when candidates borrow a class. In this situation, spend enough time with the students to understand their needs, which are foundational to your portfolio. One of the authors once watched a MoC video in which the candidate clearly had never met the students before. If she could tell, we're betting assessors could too! For more on Knowledge of Students, see Chapter 4.
- Failing to include two *distinct* PGEs. The MoC instructions specify "varied" professional experiences.
- Including Samples of Product that are not directly connected to PGEs or to positive student outcomes. The MoC instructions include a chart to help you articulate these connections.
- Featuring mediocre instruction in your video. While you have a lot of latitude in designing your lesson, showcasing solid teaching is non-negotiable! See more on this topic in Chapters 2 and 8.
- Teaching a subject other than world language. Your video should feature teaching in your original certification area.
- Overlooking required PGE criteria. PGEs will naturally lend themselves to some criteria more than others, but you need to address them all in your Written Commentary.

Drafting Your Written Commentary

It's the moment you've been waiting for: time to draft your MoC portfolio! Remember, the goal is to tie your work to improved student outcomes.

TABLE 11.1 Sentence starters and rubric checklist for MoC

Sentence starters from the prompts | PGE 1	Checklist drawn directly from the most applicable NBPTS MoC rubric points **(Please refer to the rubric for precise wording, and also note the rubric is holistic, so many points overlap with multiple prompts.)**
The need(s) I addressed in PGE 1 is/are… (Provide context: see the prompt for more detail)	___ I identify and address relevant needs of students, communities supporting students, and/or myself.
The title of PGE 1 is: Describe PGE 1:	
PGE 1 addresses the need I identified because…	
In my work on PGE 1, I deepened my content/pedagogical knowledge by… (Describe research or activities you used and how they helped)	___ I acquire and/or deepen certificate-specific content knowledge and/or pedagogical practice and/or knowledge.

(Continued)

TABLE 11.1 (*Cont.*)

My work on PGE 1 positively impacted students by… (Provide specific examples)	___ I have a meaningful, positive, direct and/or indirect impact on student learning.
Sample of Product #__ illustrates my impact on students because… (Repeat for each relevant Sample of Product)	
These are some steps, milestones, or goals I accomplished in working on PGE 1:	___ I use reflection to analyze the connections and patterns in my continuing professional growth.
One change or addition I would make in working on PGE 1 is:	
Based on this experience, my next professional step(s) will be:	

(*Continued*)

Copyright material from Erin E. H. Austin and Lisa Bartels (2026), *Achieving National Board Certification in World Languages*, Routledge

TABLE 11.1 (*Cont.*)

Sentence starters from the prompts | PGE 2	Checklist of the most applicable rubric points
The need(s) I addressed in PGE 2 is/are… (provide context: see the prompt for more detail)	___ I identify and address relevant needs of students, communities supporting students, and/or myself.
The title of PGE 2 is:	
Describe PGE 2:	
PGE 2 addresses the need I identified because…	
In my work on PGE 2, I deepened my content/pedagogical knowledge by… (Describe research or activities you used and how they helped)	___ I acquire and/or deepen certificate-specific content knowledge and/or pedagogical practice and/or knowledge.

(*Continued*)

TABLE 11.1 (*Cont.*)

My work on PGE 2 positively impacted students by… (Provide specific examples)	___ I have a meaningful, positive, direct and/or indirect impact on student learning.
Sample of Product #__ illustrates my impact on students because… (Repeat for each relevant Sample of Product	
These are some steps, milestones, or goals I accomplished in working on PGE 2:	___ I use reflection to analyze the connections and patterns in my continuing professional growth.
One change or addition I would make in working on PGE 2 is:	
Based on this experience, my next professional step(s) will be:	

(*Continued*)

TABLE 11.1 (*Cont.*)

Sentence starters from the prompts | Answer for one PGE	Checklist of the most applicable rubric points
PGE __ shows how I effectively integrate technology because…	___ I effectively integrate appropriate technology to directly and/or indirectly impact student learning.
I ensured fairness and equity of access and promoted appreciation of diversity by… (Address all three; the prompt says *and*)	___ I ensure fairness and equity of access and promote appreciation of diversity in my instructional practice.
My interaction with *(insert a person or group)* enhanced my professional growth because…	___ I involve others in Professional Growth Experiences.
As I reflect on my professional growth since certification, one pattern or theme that has emerged is… This theme defines me as an educator because…	___ I have ongoing and varied professional experiences. ___ I use reflection to analyze the connections and patterns in my continuing professional growth.

(*Continued*)

Copyright material from Erin E. H. Austin and Lisa Bartels (2026), *Achieving National Board Certification in World Languages*, Routledge

TABLE 11.1 (*Cont.*)

Sentence starters from the prompts | Component 2 (lesson recording)	Checklist of the most applicable rubric points
I applied my learning from PGE __ in this lesson by…	___ I acquire and/or deepen certificate-specific content knowledge and/or pedagogical practice and/or knowledge.
My goals for this lesson were:	___ I identify and address relevant needs of students, communities supporting students, and/or myself.
These goals fit into the broader context of these students' learning by…	
This instruction is important for these students at this particular point in time because…	
I ensured fairness and equity of access and appreciation of diversity in this lesson by… (Address all three; the prompt says *and*)	___ I ensure fairness and equity of access and appreciation of diversity.
This recording reflects my certificate-specific knowledge because…	___ I practice National Board Standards–based, relevant, and meaningful instruction in my certificate area.

(*Continued*)

Copyright material from Erin E. H. Austin and Lisa Bartels (2026), *Achieving National Board Certification in World Languages*, Routledge

TABLE 11.1 (*Cont.*)

(Specific moment in the video) reflects my impact on student learning because… (Repeat for several events in the video.)	___ I have a meaningful impact on student learning.
One change/addition that would enhance student learning is… Because…	
Based on this lesson, one change/ addition/next step to enhance my own professional growth is… Because…	___ I have ongoing and varied professional experiences. ___ I use reflection to analyze the connections and patterns in my continuing professional growth.

("Maintenance of Certification," National Board for Professional Teaching Standards 17, 21–22, 30–31). This table is downloadable from the Routledge webpage for this book, which can be found here: resourcecentre.routledge.com/books/9781041205357.

Copyright material from Erin E. H. Austin and Lisa Bartels (2026), *Achieving National Board Certification in World Languages*, Routledge

Back to the Beginning

MoC is your current finish line. Your colleagues, students, and friends are cheering you on! When you cross the line, they dump a giant bucket of Gatorade over your head! YOU DID IT! Now keep doing it, every day, every year for the rest of your career. You—and your students—are worth it.

References

National Board for Professional Teaching Standards. *Maintenance of Certification Instructions: Components 1 & 2 for All Certificate Areas.* Prepared by Pearson under contract with the National Board for Professional Teaching Standards, 2022, www.nbpts.org/wp-content/uploads/2021/05/MOC_Instructions.pdf. Accessed 7 Aug. 2025.

Glossary

ACTFL: The American Council of Teachers of Foreign Language, which governs school-based language instruction in the United States

Assessment: Any activity used to gauge students' current knowledge or ability

- ♦ **Formative assessment**: an assessment used before instruction to provide information about what students already know or can do
- ♦ **Summative assessment**: an assessment used at the end of an instructional sequence to provide information about student mastery of the instructional goals

Authentic resource: Content that was created by target-language speakers for target-language speakers. Some definitions include materials that have been translated by and for target-language speakers (e.g., a Hollywood film that has been dubbed).

Backwards design: developing an instructional sequence by identifying unit goals, then developing an assessment for those goals, and then planning instruction to prepare students for that assessment

Bloom's Taxonomy: a framework to categorize learning tasks from most simple to most complex

Comprehensible input: any listening or reading in the target language which the learner can understand (with or without aids)

Differentiation: providing more than one instructional pathway for different students to meet the same objective

Instructional practice: everything a teacher does to impact student learning

Instructional sequence: an intentional and tailored series of lessons guiding students toward a specific goal

Language acquisition: an unconscious process of developing proficiency through multiple exposures to comprehensible input

Modes of communication: The ways in which communication takes place. There are two models for this.

1. reading/writing/listening/speaking. Reading and writing represent written communication, while listening and speaking are verbal. Reading and listening involve receptive language, while writing and speaking are productive tasks.
2. ACTFL identifies three modes of communication:
    - **Interpretive:** understanding language input. Interpretive tasks can involve reading or listening and require receptive language.
    - **Interpersonal:** an exchange of information between two or more people. Interpersonal tasks can be oral or written and require both receptive and productive language.
    - **Presentational:** providing information to an audience through speaking or writing. Presentational tasks involve productive language.

Modeling: demonstrating desired outcomes

Pedagogy: a teacher's understanding of how to teach and how students learn

Proficiency: the ability to read, write, listen, and speak appropriately in the target language

Proficiency-based: focused on communicative skills, rather than on isolated language components

Realia: real products from a target culture

Recasting: a form of modeling where the teacher restates a phrase correctly after a student error, without directly correcting the student

Scaffolding: intentionally and gradually removing instructional supports to help students develop more independence

Spiraling: a technique in which teachers continually circle back to previously taught concepts, connecting them and weaving them into new (and more complex) learning

Standard: a description of what learners (or teachers) should know and be able to do

- ACTFL standards: expected outcomes for language learners, organized around the 5 C's: Communication, Cultures, Connections, Comparisons, and Communities. ACTFL standards govern language teaching in the United States
- NBPTS standards: a description of what National Board Certified Teachers should know and be able to do
- State standards: state-specific expected student outcomes

Target cultures: cultures where the language students are learning is spoken

Target language (TL): the language students are learning

Validity (of an assessment): the degree to which an assessment measures what it is intended to measure, and nothing else

Resources

American Council on the Teaching of Foreign Languages (ACTFL): https://www.actfl.org/

    Standards & 5 C's: https://tinyurl.com/re9jcrsx
    3 P's: https://tinyurl.com/ykmhrf89

Facebook groups:

    National Board Certification for World Language Teachers
    National Board Certification Survival Group
    National Board Certified Teachers on Facebook
    MOC for World Languages
    NBCT Support
    Teachers Undergoing National Board Certification

National Board for Professional Teaching Standards: https://www.nbpts.org/

Architecture of Accomplished Teaching: https://tinyurl.com/yc7n3yy3

Component resources: https://tinyurl.com/yxcdphh3

Five Core Propositions: https://www.nbpts.org/certification/five-core-propositions/

Language Proficiency Requirements: https://tinyurl.com/szej35m3

Maintenance of Certification: https://tinyurl.com/2s3v796m

Standards for WL: https://www.nbpts.org/certification/standards/

Podcast: National Board Conversations

https://www.nbpts.org/podcast/

YouTube channel: https://www.youtube.com/@erin-eh-austin

Video: Achieving National Board Certification as a World Language Teacher
https://youtu.be/q2j68roaE48
Video: National Board Certification: Component 1 (World Language)
https://youtu.be/4Rj17PJPEG4
Video: National Board Certification: Component 2 (World Language)
https://youtu.be/DXug854oiIc
Video: National Board Certification: Component 3 (World Language)
https://youtu.be/PpAvk-zMzD0
Video: National Board Certification: Component 4 (World Language)
https://youtu.be/QRPIRGp1_KM

For Product Safety Concerns and Information please contact our EU
representative GPSR@taylorandfrancis.com
Taylor & Francis Verlag GmbH, Kaufingerstraße 24, 80331 München, Germany

www.ingramcontent.com/pod-product-compliance
Lightning Source LLC
Chambersburg PA
CBHW061441300426
44114CB00014B/1784